DK LANGUAGE LEARNER

French
2,000-word
Bilingual Dictionary

LONDON, NEW YORK, MELBOURNE,
MUNICH, and DELHI

Contents

London, New York,
Melbourne, Munich, and Delhi

Senior Editor Hazel Beynon

Senior Art Editor Smiljka Surla

Editor Jenny Finch

Designer Marilou Prokopiou

Managing Editor Linda Esposito

Managing Art Editor
Diane Thistlethwaite

Publishing Manager Andrew Macintyre

Category Publisher Laura Buller

Production Controller Erica Rosen

DTP Designer Siu Chan

Jacket Designer Neal Cobourne

Jacket Editor Mariza O'Keeffe

Written by Viv Lambert

Consultant Suzanne Gaynor

Pronunciation Guide Elise Bradbury

This edition published in the
United States in 2006 by
DK Publishing, Inc.
375 Hudson Street, New York, New York 10014

06 07 08 09 10 10 9 8 7 6 5 4 3 2 1

DK Books are available at special discounts for sales
promotions, premiums, fund-raising, or educational use.
For details, contact: DK Publishing Special Markets,
375 Hudson Street, New York, New York 10014
SpecialSales@dk.com

A catalog record for this book is available from the
Library of Congress.

ISBN-13: 978-0-75662-071-4
ISBN-10: 0-7566-2071-6

Color reproduction by Icon, UK
Printed by Imago, China

Discover more at
www.dk.com

How to use this dictionary

In the first section, the English words are given in alphabetical order, with the French translation and pronunciation. A guide to French pronunciation is provided on page 51. In the second section, you'll find the French words together with their English translation. The verbs are in a separate section. At the back of the book, there is a list of useful phrases that you can use when you practice speaking French with your friends.

This shows the first letter of the words on the page

English entry word

French translation

First word on the page with the French translation

French pronunciation

Last word on the page with the French translation

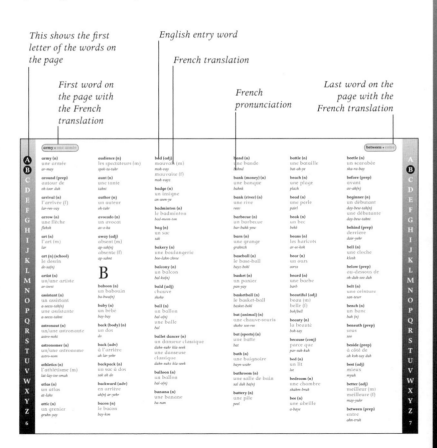

A
B

army (n)
une armée
ar-may

around (prep)
autour de
oh-toor duh

arrival (n)
l'arrivée (f)
lar-ree-vay

arrow (n)
une flèche
flehsh

art (n)
l'art (m)
lar

art (n) (school)
le dessin
de-sa(n)

artist (n)
un/une artiste
ar-teest

assistant (n)
un assistant
a-seess-tah(n)
une assistante
a-seess-tahnt

astronaut (n)
un/une astronaute
astro-noht

astronomer (n)
un/une astronome
astro-nom

athletics (n)
l'athlétisme (m)
lat-lay-tee-smah

atlas (n)
un atlas
at-lahs

attic (n)
un grenier
gruhn-yay

audience (n)
les spectateurs (m)
spek-ta-tuhr

aunt (n)
une tante
tahnt

author (n)
un auteur
oh-tuhr

avocado (n)
un avocat
av-o-ka

away (adj)
absent (m)
ap-suh(n)
absente (f)
ap-sahnt

B

baboon (n)
un babouin
ba-bwa(n)

baby (n)
un bébé
bay-bay

back (body) (n)
un dos
do

back (adv)
à l'arrière
ah lar-yehr

backpack (n)
un sac à dos
sak ah do

backward (adv)
en arrière
ah(n) ar-yehr

bacon (n)
le bacon
bay-kon

bad (adj)
mauvais (m)
moh-vay
mauvaise (f)
moh-vayz

badge (n)
un insigne
an-seen-ye

badminton (n)
le badminton
bad-meen-ton

bag (n)
un sac
sak

bakery (n)
une boulangerie
boo-lahn-zhree

balcony (n)
un balcon
bal-ko(n)

bald (adj)
chauve
shohv

ball (n)
un ballon
bal-o(n)
une balle
bal

ballet dancer (n)
un danseur classique
dahn-suhr kla-seek
une danseuse
classique
dahn-suhz kla-seek

balloon (n)
un ballon
bal-o(n)

banana (n)
une banane
ba-nan

band (n)
une bande
bähnd

bank (money) (n)
une banque
bahnk

bank (river) (n)
une rive
reev

barbecue (n)
un barbecue
bar-buhk-yew

barn (n)
une grange
grahnzh

baseball (n)
le base-ball
bays-bohl

basket (n)
un panier
pan-yay

basketball (n)
le basket-ball
basket-bohl

bat (animal) (n)
une chauve-souris
shohv soo-ree

bat (sports) (n)
une batte
bat

bath (n)
une baignoire
bayn-wahr

bathroom (n)
une salle de bain
sal duh ba(n)

battery (n)
une pile
peel

battle (n)
une bataille
bat-ah-ye

beach (n)
une plage
plazh

bead (n)
une perle
pairl

beak (n)
un bec
behk

beans (n)
les haricots
ar-ee-koh

bear (n)
un ours
oorss

beard (n)
une barbe
barb

beautiful (adj)
beau (m)
boh
belle (f)
bohl/bell

beauty (n)
la beauté
boh-tay

because (conj)
parce que
par-suh-kuh

bed (n)
un lit
lee

bedroom (n)
une chambre
shahm-bruh

bee (n)
une abeille
a-baye

beetle (n)
un scarabée
ska-ra-bay

before (prep)
avant
av-ah(n)

beginner (n)
un debutant
day-bew-tah(n)
une débutante
day-bew-tahnt

behind (prep)
derrière
dair-yehr

bell (n)
une cloche
klosh

below (prep)
au-dessous de
oh-duh-soo duh

belt (n)
une ceinture
san-tewr

bench (n)
un banc
bah (n)

beneath (prep)
sous
soo

beside (prep)
à côté de
ah koh-tay duh

best (adj)
mieux
myuh

better (adj)
meilleur (m)
may-yuhr
meilleure (f)
may-yuhr

between (prep)
entre
ahn-truh

6

7

3

A
B
C
D
E
F
G
H
I
J
K
L
M
N
O
P
Q
R
S
T
U
V
W
X
Y
Z

English A–Z

In this section, the English words are given in alphabetical order, followed by the French translation. There is information after each English word to show you what type of word it is. In French, nouns (naming words) are either masculine or feminine. If the French word has **un** before it, it is masculine (m); if it has **une**, it is feminine (f).

(n) = noun (a naming word). Nouns are either masculine or feminine. Feminine nouns usually have an "e" at the end.

(adj) = adjective (a describing word). These words can change depending on whether the noun they are describing is masculine (m) or feminine (f).

(adv) = adverb (a word that gives more information about a verb, an adjective, or another adverb).

(conj) = conjunction (a joining word, e.g., *and*).

(prep) = preposition (e.g., *about*).

(pron) = pronoun (e.g., *he*, *she*, *it*).

(article) = (e.g., *a, an, the*).

A

a (article)
un/une
a(n)/ewn

about (adv)
environ
ahn-veer-o(n)

about (prep)
sur
soor

above (prep)
au-dessus de
oh duhs-ew duh

accident (n)
un accident
ak-see-dah(n)

acrobat (n)
un/une acrobate
ak-ro-bat

across (prep)
de l'autre côté de
duh loh-truh koh-tay duh

action (n)
une action
ak-syo(n)

activity (n)
une activité
ak-tee-vee-tay

actor (n)
un acteur (m)
ak-tuhr

actress (n)
une actrice (f)
ak-treess

address (n)
une adresse
a-dress

adult (n)
un/une adulte
ad-ewlt

adventure (n)
une aventure
av-ahn-tewr

after (prep)
après
ap-reh

afternoon (n)
un après-midi
ap-reh mee-dee

again (adv)
encore
ahn-kor

against (prep)
contre
kon-truh

age (n)
l'âge (m)
lahzh

ahead (prep)
devant
duh-vah(n)

air (n)
l'air (m)
lair

airplane (n)
un avion
av-yo(n)

airport (n)
un aéroport
a-ay-ro-por

alarm clock (n)
un réveil
ray-vaye

alien (n)
un/une extraterrestre
ek-stra-tair-es-truh

alive (adj)
vivant (m)
vivante (f)
vee-vah(n)/vee-vahnt

all (adj)
tout (m) toute (f)
too/toot

alligator (n)
un alligator
al-ee-gah-tor

allowance (n)
l'argent de poche (m)
lar-zhah(n) duh posh

almost (adv)
presque
presk

alone (adj)
seul (m) seule (f)
suhl

alphabet (n)
l'alphabet (m)
lal-fa-bay

already (adv)
déjà
day-zha

also (adv)
aussi
oh-see

although (conj)
bien que
bya(n) kuh

always (adv)
toujours
too-zhoor

amazing (adj)
incroyable
an-krwa-ya-bluh

ambulance (n)
une ambulance
ahm-bew-lahnss

among (prep)
entre
ahn-truh

amount (n)
une quantité
kahn-tee-tay

an (article)
un/une
a(n)/ewn

anchor (n)
une ancre
ahn-kruh

and (conj)
et
eh

angry (adj)
en colère
ah(n) ko-lehr

animal (n)
un animal
an-ee-mal

ankle (n)
une cheville
shuh-vee-ye

another (adj)
autre
oh-truh

answer (n)
une réponse
ray-ponss

ant (n)
une fourmi
foor-mee

antenna (n)
une antenne
ahn-ten

anybody (pron)
n'importe qui
nam-port kee

anything (pron)
n'importe quoi
nam-port kwa

apart (adv)
séparément
say-pa-ray-mah(n)

apartment (n)
un appartement
ap-par-tuh-mah(n)

ape (n)
un singe (m)
sanzh

appearance (n)
une apparence
ap-par-ahnss

apple (n)
une pomme
pom

apple juice (n)
un jus de pomme
zhew duh pom

apricot (n)
un abricot
ab-ree-koh

apron (n)
un tablier
tab-lee-yay

arch (n)
une arche
arsh

architect (n)
un/une architecte
ar-shee-tekt

area (n)
une région
ray-zhyo(n)

arm (n)
un bras
bra

armchair (n)
un fauteuil
foh-tuh-ye

A
B
C
D
E
F
G
H
I
J
K
L
M
N
O
P
Q
R
S
T
U
V
W
X
Y
Z

A
B
C
D
E
F
G
H
I
J
K
L
M
N
O
P
Q
R
S
T
U
V
W
X
Y
Z

army (n)
une armée
ar-may

around (prep)
autour de
oh-toor duh

arrival (n)
l'arrivée (f)
lar-ree-vay

arrow (n)
une flèche
flehsh

art (n)
l'art (m)
lar

art (n) (school)
le dessin
de-sa(n)

artist (n)
un/une artiste
ar-teest

assistant (n)
un assistant
a-seess-tah(n)
une assistante
a-seess-tahnt

astronaut (n)
un/une astronaute
astro-noht

astronomer (n)
un/une astronome
astro-nom

athletics (n)
l'athlétisme (m)
lat-lay-tee-smah

atlas (n)
un atlas
at-lahs

attic (n)
un grenier
gruhn-yay

audience (n)
les spectateurs (m)
spek-ta-tuhr

aunt (n)
une tante
tahnt

author (n)
un auteur
oh-tuhr

avocado (n)
un avocat
av-o-ka

away (adj)
absent (m)
ap-sah(n)
absente (f)
ap-sahnt

B

baboon (n)
un babouin
ba-bwa(n)

baby (n)
un bébé
bay-bay

back (body) (n)
un dos
do

back (adv)
à l'arrière
ah lar-yehr

backpack (n)
un sac à dos
sak ah do

backward (adv)
en arrière
ah(n) ar-yehr

bacon (n)
le bacon
bay-kon

bad (adj)
mauvais (m)
moh-vay
mauvaise (f)
moh-vayz

badge (n)
un insigne
an-seen-ye

badminton (n)
le badminton
bad-meen-ton

bag (n)
un sac
sak

bakery (n)
une boulangerie
boo-lahn-zhree

balcony (n)
un balcon
bal-ko(n)

bald (adj)
chauve
shohv

ball (n)
un ballon
bal-o(n)
une balle
bal

ballet dancer (n)
un danseur classique
dahn-suhr kla-seek
une danseuse
classique
dahn-suhz kla-seek

balloon (n)
un ballon
bal-o(n)

banana (n)
une banane
ba-nan

band (n)
une bande
bahnd

bank (money) (n)
une banque
bahnk

bank (river) (n)
une rive
reev

barbecue (n)
un barbecue
bar-buhk-yew

barn (n)
une grange
grahnzh

baseball (n)
le base-ball
bayz-bohl

basket (n)
un panier
pan-yay

basketball (n)
le basket-ball
basket-bohl

bat (animal) (n)
une chauve-souris
shohv soo-ree

bat (sports) (n)
une batte
bat

bath (n)
une baignoire
bayn-wahr

bathroom (n)
une salle de bain
sal duh ba(n)

battery (n)
une pile
peel

battle (n)
une bataille
bat-ah-ye

beach (n)
une plage
plazh

bead (n)
une perle
pairl

beak (n)
un bec
behk

beans (n)
les haricots
ar-ee-koh

bear (n)
un ours
oorss

beard (n)
une barbe
barb

beautiful (adj)
beau (m)
belle (f)
boh/bell

beauty (n)
la beauté
boh-tay

because (conj)
parce que
par-suh-kuh

bed (n)
un lit
lee

bedroom (n)
une chambre
shahm-bruh

bee (n)
une abeille
a-baye

beetle (n)
un scarabée
ska-ra-bay

before (prep)
avant
av-ah(n)

beginner (n)
un débutant
day-bew-tah(n)
une débutante
day-bew-tahnt

behind (prep)
derrière
dair-yehr

bell (n)
une cloche
klosh

below (prep)
au-dessous de
oh-duh-soo duh

belt (n)
une ceinture
san-tewr

bench (n)
un banc
bah (n)

beneath (prep)
sous
soo

beside (prep)
à côté de
ah koh-tay duh

best (adj)
mieux
myuh

better (adj)
meilleur (m)
meilleure (f)
may-yuhr

between (prep)
entre
ahn-truh

A
B
C
D
E
F
G
H
I
J
K
L
M
N
O
P
Q
R
S
T
U
V
W
X
Y
Z

7

beverage (n)
une boisson
bwa-so(n)

big (large) (adj)
gros (m)
grosse (f)
groh/grohss

big (tall) (adj)
grand (m)
grah(n)
grande (f)
grahnd

bike (n)
un vélo
vay-lo

bill (n)
une addition
ad-dee-syo(n)

billion
milliard
meel-yar

bin (n)
une poubelle
poo-bell

binoculars (n)
les jumelles
zhew-mel

bird (n)
un oiseau
wa-zoh

birthday (n)
un anniversaire
an-ee-vair-sair

birthday cake (n)
un gâteau
d'anniversaire
gah-toh dan-ee-vair-sair

birthday card (n)
une carte
d'anniversaire
kart dan-ee-vair-sair

biscuit (n)
un biscuit
bee-skwee

bitter (adj)
amer (m) amère (f)
am-air

black (adj)
noir (m)
noire (f)
nwahr

blackboard (n)
un tableau
tab-loh

blanket (n) (f)
une couverture
koo-vair-tewr

blocks (n)
les cubes
kewb

blonde (adj)
blond (m)
bloh(n)
blonde (f)
blohnd

blood (n)
le sang
sah(n)

blouse (n)
un chemisier
shuh-meez-yay

blue (adj)
bleu (m)
bleue (f)
bluh

board (notice) (n)
un panneau
pan-noh

board game (n)
un jeu de société
zhuh duh soh-see-ay-tay

boat (n)
un bateau
ba-toh

body (n)
un corps
kor

bone (n)
un os
oss

book (n)
un livre
leev-ruh

book bag (n)
un cartable
kar-ta-bluh

bookstore (n)
une librairie
leeb-rair-ee

boot (n)
une botte
bot

boring (adj)
ennuyeux (m)
ahn-wee-yuh
ennuyeuse (f)
ahn-wee-yuhz

bottle (n)
une bouteille
boo-taye

bottom (n)
le fond
foh(n)

bowl (cereal) (n)
un bol
bol

box (n)
une boîte
bwat

boy (n)
un garçon
gar-so(n)

boyfriend (n)
un petit ami
puh-tee-ta-mee

bracelet (n)
un bracelet
bra-slay

brain (n)
un cerveau
sair-voh

branch (n)
une branche
brahnsh

brave (adj)
courageux (m)
koor-a-zhuh
courageuse (f)
koor-a-zhuhz

bread (n)
le pain
pa(n)

break (n)
une pause
pohz

breakfast (n)
le petit-déjeuner
puh-tee day-zhuh-nay

breath (n)
un souffle
soo-fluh

breeze (n)
une brise
breez

bridge (n)
un pont
po(n)

bright (adj)
brillant (m)
bree-yah(n)
brillante (f)
bree-yahnt

broken (adj)
cassé (m)
cassée (f)
kah-say

broom (n)
un balai
ba-lay

brother (n)
un frère
frair

brown (adj)
marron
mar-o(n)

bruise (n)
un bleu
bluh

bubble (n)
une bulle
bewl

bucket (n)
un seau
soh

bug (illness) (n)
un microbe
meek-rohb

bug (insect) (n)
un insecte
an-sekt

buggy (stroller) (n)
une poussette
poo-set

building (n)
un bâtiment
bah-tee-mah(n)

bulb (light) (n)
une ampoule
ahm-pool

bulb (plant) (n)
un bulbe
bewlb

bunk beds (n)
les lits superposés (m)
lee soo-pair-poh-zay

buoy (n)
une bouée
boo-way

bus (n)
un autobus
ohto-bews

bus stop (n)
un arrêt de bus
ar-reh duh bews

bush (n)
un buisson
bwee-so(n)

business (n)
les affaires
a-fair

busy (adj)
occupé (m)
occupée (f)
ok-ew-pay

but (conj)
mais
may

butcher's shop (n)
une boucherie
boosh-ree

butter (n)
le beurre
buhr

butterfly (n)
un papillon
pa-pee-yo(n)

button (n)
un bouton
boo-to(n)

A B C D E F G H I J K L M N O P Q R S T U V W X Y Z

9

A
B
C
D
E
F
G
H
I
J
K
L
M
N
O
P
Q
R
S
T
U
V
W
X
Y
Z

10

C

cabbage (n)
un chou
shoo

café (n)
un café
ka-fay

cage (n)
une cage
kahzh

cake (n)
un gâteau
gah-toh

calculator (n)
une calculatrice
kal-kew-la-treess

calendar (n)
un calendrier
kal-ahn-dree-yay

calf (n)
un veau
voh

calm (adj)
calme
kalm

camel (n)
un chameau
sha-moh

camera (n)
un appareil
photo
ap-pa-ray fo-toh

campsite (n)
un camping
kahm-peeng

can (n)
un bidon
bee-do(n)

candle (n)
une bougie
boo-zhee

canoe (n)
un canoë
kan-o-ay

cap (n)
une casquette
kas-ket

capital (n)
une capitale
ka-pee-tal

car (n)
une voiture
vwah-tewr

caravan (n)
une caravane
ka-ra-van

carbonated (adj)
gazeux (m)
gaz-uh
gazeuse (f)
gaz-uhz

card (n)
une carte
kart

cardboard (n)
le carton
kar-to(n)

cards (n)
les cartes
kart

careful (adj)
prudent (m)
prew-dah(n)
prudente (f)
prew-dahnt

carnival (n)
un carnaval
kar-na-val

carpet (n)
une moquette
moh-ket

carrot (n)
une carotte
ka-rot

cart (supermarket) (n)
un caddie
ka-dee

cart (n)
une charrette
sha-ret

cartoon (drawing) (n)
une bande
dessinée
bahnd dess-ee-nay

cartoon (movie) (n)
un dessin animé
de-san an-ee-may

**cartwheel
(movement) (n)**
une roue
roo

cash (n)
en espèces
ah(n) es-pehss

cash register (n)
une caisse
kess

cassette (n)
une cassette
ka-set

castle (n)
un château
sha-toh

cat (n)
un chat
sha

caterpillar (n)
une chenille
shuh-nee-ye

cathedral (n)
une cathédrale
ka-tay-dral

cattle (n)
le bétail
bay-tye

cauliflower (n)
un chou-fleur
shoo-fluhr

cave (n)
une grotte
grot

CD (n)
un CD
say-day

CD player (n)
un lecteur de CD
lek-tuhr duh say-day

ceiling (n)
le plafond
pla-fo(n)

celebration (n)
une célébration
say-lay-bra-syo(n)

cellar (n)
une cave
kav

cell phone (n)
un téléphone
portable/
un portable
tay-lay-fon por-ta-bluh

center (n)
le centre
sahn-truh

cereal (n)
une céréale
sair-ay-al

certain (adj)
certain (m)
sair-ta(n)
certaine (f)
sair-tehn

chain (n)
une chaîne
shehn

chair (n)
une chaise
shehz

challenge (n)
un défi
day-fee

chance (n)
une chance
shahns

change (n)
un changement
shahnzh-mah(n)

change purse (n)
un porte-monnaie
port-mo-nay

cheap (adj)
bon marché
bo(n) mar-shay

checkout (n)
une caisse
kehss

cheek (body) (n)
la joue
zhoo

cheese (n)
un fromage
fro-mazh

cheetah (n)
un guépard
gay-par

chef (n)
un/une chef
shef

cherry (n)
une cerise
sair-eez

chess (n)
les échecs
ay-shek

chest (n)
une poitrine
pwa-treen

chest of drawers (n)
une commode
kom-mod

chewing gum (n)
un chewing-gum
shweeng gom

chick (n)
un poussin
poo-sa(n)

chicken (n)
un poulet
poo-lay

child (n)
un/une enfant
ahn-fah(n)

children (n)
les enfants
ahn-fah(n)

chimney (n)
une cheminée
shuh-mee-nay

chimpanzee (n)
un chimpanzé
shahm-pahn-zay

chin (n)
un menton
mahn-to(n)

chocolate (n)
le chocolat
sho-ko-la

choice (n)
un choix
shwa

A B C D E F G H I J K L M N O P Q R S T U V W X Y Z

Christmas (n)
Noël
no-el

church (n)
une église
ayg-leess

circle (n)
un cercle
sair-kluh

circus (n)
un cirque
seerk

city (n)
une ville
veel

class (school) (n)
une classe
klass

classroom (n)
une salle de
classe
sal duh klahss

claw (n)
une griffe
greef

clean (adj)
propre
prop-ruh

clear (adj)
clair (m)
claire (f)
klair

clever (adj)
intelligent (m)
an-tel-lee-zhah(n)
intelligente (f)
an-tel-lee-zhahnt

cliff (n)
une falaise
fa-lehz

cloak (n)
une cape
kap

clock (n)
une horloge
or-lozh

close (near) (adj)
proche
prosh

closed (adj)
fermé (m) fermée (f)
fair-may

cloth (n)
un tissu
tee-soo

clothes (n)
les vêtements
veht-mah(n)

cloud (n)
un nuage
new-azh

cloudy (adj)
nuageux (m)
new-azh-uh
nuageuse (f)
new-azh-uhz

clown (n)
un clown
kloon

club (n)
un club
kluhb

clumsy (adj)
maladroit (m)
mal-a-drwa
maladroite (f)
mal-a-drwat

coast (n)
une côte
koht

coat (n)
un manteau
mahn-toh

coat hanger (n)
un cintre
san-truh

coffee (n)
le café
ka-fay

coin (n)
une pièce
pyehs

cold (adj)
froid (m)
frwa
froide (f)
frwad

cold (n)
un rhume
rewm

collar (n)
un collier
kol-yay

color (n)
une couleur
koo-luhr

colored pencil (n)
un crayon de
couleur
kra-yo(n) duh koo-luhr

colorful (adj)
coloré (m)
colorée (f)
ko-lo-ray

comb (n)
un peigne
pain-ye

combine harvester (n)
une moissonneuse-
batteuse
mwa-son-nuhz bat-tuhz

comfortable (adj)
confortable
kon-for-ta-bluh

comforter (n)
une couette
koo-et

comic (n)
un comique
ko-meek

compass (n)
une boussole
boo-sol

competition (n)
une compétition
kom-pay-tee-syo(n)

computer (n)
un ordinateur
or-dee-na-tuhr

computer game (n)
un jeu électronique
zhuh ay-lek-tro-neek

concert (n)
un concert
kon-sair

construction worker (n)
un ouvrier
oov-ree-yay
une ouvrière
oov-ree-yair

continent (n)
un continent
kon-tee-nah(n)

controls (n)
les commandes
ko-mahnd

conversation (n)
une conversation
kon-vair-sa-syo(n)

cool (adj)
frais (m)
fray

fraîche (f)
frehsh

corner (n)
un coin
kwa(n)

correct (adj)
juste
zhewst

corridor (n)
un couloir
kool-wahr

costume (n)
un costume
kos-tewm

cotton (n)
le coton
ko-to(n)

cough (n)
une toux
too

country (n)
un pays
pay-ee

countryside (n)
la campagne
kahm-pan-ye

cousin (n)
un cousin
koo-za(n)
une cousine
koo-zeen

cow (n)
une vache
vash

cowboy (n)
un cow-boy
koh-boye

crab (n)
un crabe
krab

crane (n)
une grue
grew

crayon (n)
un crayon de couleur
kray-o(n) duh koo-luhr

crazy (adj)
fou (m)
foo
folle (f)
fol

cream (n)
la crème
krehm

creature (n)
une bête
beht

crew (n)
l'équipage (m)
ay-kee-pazh

crocodile (n)
un crocodile
kro-ko-deel

crop (n)
une récolte
ray-kolt

crossing (n)
un carrefour
kar-foor

crosswalk (n)
un passage clouté
pa-sazh kloo-tay

crowd (n)
la foule
fool

crowded (adj)
bondé (m)
bondée (f)
bon-day

A
B
C
D
E
F
G
H
I
J
K
L
M
N
O
P
Q
R
S
T
U
V
W
X
Y
Z

A
B
C
D
E
F
G
H
I
J
K
L
M
N
O
P
Q
R
S
T
U
V
W
X
Y
Z

crown (n)
une couronne
koo-ron

cruel (adj)
cruel (m)
cruelle (f)
krew-ell

cube (n)
un cube
kewb

cucumber (n)
un concombre
kon-kom-bruh

cup (n)
une tasse
tahss

cupboard (n)
un placard
pla-kar

cupboard (tall) (n)
une armoire
arm-wahr

curious (adj)
curieux (m)
kew-ree-uh
curieuse (f)
kew-ree-uhz

curly (adj)
frisé (m) frisée (f)
free-zay

curtain (n)
un rideau
ree-doh

curved (adj)
courbé(e)
koor-bay

cushion (n)
un coussin
koo-sa(n)

customer (n)
un client
klee-ah(n)
une cliente
klee-ahnt

D

dad (n)
papa
pa-pa

dairy (adj)
laitier (m) laitière (f)
layt-yay/layt-yair

daisy (n)
une pâquerette
pak-uh-ret

dancer (n)
un danseur
dahn-suhr
une danseuse
dahn-suhz

dandelion (n)
un pissenlit
pee-sahn-lee

danger (n)
le danger
dahn-zhay

dangerous (adj)
dangereux (m)
dahn-zhay-ruh
dangereuse (f)
dahn-zhay-ruhz

dark (adj)
sombre
som-bruh

dark (hair) (adj)
foncé (m)
foncée (f)
fon-say

date (n)
une date
dat

daughter (n)
une fille
fee-ye

day (n)
un jour
zhoor

dawn (n)
l'aube (f)
lohb

dead (adj)
mort (m) morte (f)
mor/mort

deaf (adj)
sourd (m) sourde (f)
soor/soord

dear (special, expensive) (adj)
cher (m) chère (f)
shair

deck (boat) (n)
un pont
po(n)

deck chair (n)
une chaise longue
shayz long-uh

decoration (n)
une décoration
day-ko-ra-syo(n)

deep (adj)
profond (m)
pro-fo(n)
profonde (f)
pro-fond

deer (n)
un daim
da(m)

delicious (adj)
délicieux (m)
day-lee-syuh

délicieuse (f)
day-lee-syuhz

dentist (n)
un/une dentiste
dahn-teest

desert (n)
un désert
day-zair

desk (n)
un bureau
bew-roh

dessert (n)
un dessert
duh-sair

detective (n)
un détective
day-tek-teev

diagram (n)
un diagramme
dya-gram

diamond (shape) (n)
un losange
lo-zahnzh

diary (n)
un journal
zhoor-nal

dice (n)
les dés
day

dictionary (n)
un dictionnaire
deek-syo-nair

different (adj)
différent (m)
dee-fay-rah(n)
différente (f)
dee-fay-rahnt

difficult (adj)
difficile
dee-fee-seel

digital (adj)
digital (m)
digitale (f)
dee-zhee-tal

dining room (n)
une salle à manger
sal ah mahn-zhay

dinner (n)
un dîner
dee-nay

dinosaur (n)
un dinosaure
dee-noh-zor

direction (n)
une direction
dee-rek-syo(n)

directly (adv)
directement
dee-rek-tuh-mah(n)

dirty (adj)
sale
sal

disabled (adj)
handicapé (m)
handicapée (f)
ahn-dee-ka-pay

disaster (n)
une catastrophe
ka-ta-strof

disco (n)
une discothèque
dee-sko-tek

disease (n)
une maladie
ma-la-dee

disguise (n)
un déguisement
day-gheez-mah(n)

dishes (dirty) (n)
la vaisselle
vay-sel

dish towel (n)
un torchon
tor-sho(n)

dishwasher (n)
un lave-vaisselle
lav vay-sel

distance (n)
une distance
dee-stahnss

diving (n)
la plongée
plon-zhay

divorced (adj)
divorcé (m)
divorcée (f)
dee-vor-say

doctor (n)
un médecin
may-duh-sa(n)

doctor's office (n)
un cabinet médical
ka-bee-nay may-dee-kal

dog (n)
un chien
shya(n)

doll (n)
une poupée
poo-pay

dolphin (n)
un dauphin
doh-fa(n)

dome (n)
un dôme
dohm

door (n)
une porte
port

downstairs (adv)
au rez-de-chaussée
oh ray-du-shoh-say

A
B
C
D
E
F
G
H
I
J
K
L
M
N
O
P
Q
R
S
T
U
V
W
X
Y
Z

dragon (n)
un dragon
dra-go(n)

dragonfly (n)
une libellule
lee-bel-lewl

drawer (n)
un tiroir
teer-wahr

drawing (act of) (n)
le dessin
de-sa(n)

dream (n)
un rêve
rehv

dress (n)
une robe
rob

drop (n)
une goutte
goot

drum (n)
un tambour
tahm-boor

drum set (n)
une batterie
bat-tree

dry (adj)
sec (m) sèche (f)
sek/sehsh

duck (n)
un canard
ka-nar

duckling (n)
un caneton
ka-nuh-to(n)

during (prep)
pendant
pahn-dah(n)

dusk (n)
le crépuscule (m)
kray-pew-skewl

dust (n)
la poussière
poo-syair

DVD (n)
un DVD
day-vay-day

DVD player (n)
un lecteur de DVD
lek-tuhr duh day-vay-day

E

each (adj)
chaque
shak

eagle (n)
un aigle
ay-gluh

ear (n)
une oreille
o-raye

earache (n)
une otite
o-teet

early (adv)
tôt
toh

earring (n)
une boucle d'oreille
book-luh do-raye

Earth (planet) (n)
la Terre
tair

earthquake (n)
un tremblement de
terre
*trahm-bluh-mah(n)
duh tair*

earthworm (n)
un ver de terre
vair duh tair

east (n)
l'est (m)
lest

easy (adj)
facile
fa-seel

echo (n)
un écho
ay-ko

edge (n)
le bord
bor

education (n)
l'éducation (f)
lay-dew-ka-syo(n)

effect (n)
un effet
ay-fay

egg (n)
un œuf
uhf

elbow (n)
un coude
kood

electrical (adj)
électrique
ay-lek-treek

electricity (n)
l'électricité (f)
lay-lek-tree-see-tay

elephant (n)
un éléphant
ay-lay-fah(n)

elevator (n)
un ascenseur
a-sahn-suhr

email (n)
un e-mail
ee-mail

email address (n)
une adresse
électronique
a-dress ay-lek-tro-neek

emergency (n)
une urgence
ewr-zhahnss

empty (adj)
vide
veed

encyclopedia (n)
une encyclopédie
ahn-see-klo-pay-dee

end (final part) (n)
la fin
fa(n)

enemy (n)
un ennemi
une ennemie
en-mee

energy (n)
l'énergie (f)
lay-nair-zhee

English (n)
l'anglais (m)
lahn-glay

enormous (adj)
énorme
ay-norm

enough (adj)
assez
a-say

enthusiastic (adj)
enthousiaste
ahn-too-zee-ast

entrance (n)
l'entrée (f)
ahn-tray

envelope (n)
une enveloppe
ahn-vlop

environment (n)
l'environnement (m)
lahn-vee-ron-mah(n)

equal (adj)
égal (m) égale (f)
ay-gal

equator (n)
l'équateur (m)
lay-kwa-tuhr

equipment (n)
le matériel
ma-tay-ree-el

eraser (n)
une gomme
gom

even (adv)
même
mehm

evening (n)
un soir
swahr

event (n)
un événement
ay-vayn-mah(n)

every (adj)
tous
too

everybody (pron)
tout le monde
too luh mond

everyday (adv)
tous les jours
too lay zhoor

everything (pron)
tout
too

everywhere (adv)
partout
par-too

evil (adj)
mauvais (m)
moh-vay
mauvaise (f)
moh-vayz

exactly (adv)
exactement
eg-zak-tuh-mah(n)

exam (n)
un examen
eg-za-ma(n)

example (n)
un exemple
eg-zahm-pluh

excellent (adj)
excellent (m)
ek-say-lah(n)
excellente (f)
ek-say-lahnt

exchange (n)
un échange
ay-shahnzh

excited (adj)
excité (m)
excitée (f)
ek-see-tay

exercise (n)
un exercice
ek-sair-seess

excuse (n)
une excuse
ek-skewz

exhibition (n)
une exposition
ek-spoh-zee-syo(n)

exit (n)
la sortie
sor-tee

expedition (n)
une expédition
ek-spay-dee-syo(n)

A
B
C
D
E
F
G
H
I
J
K
L
M
N
O
P
Q
R
S
T
U
V
W
X
Y
Z

17

expensive (adj)
cher (m) chère (f)
shair

experiment (n)
une expérience
ek-spay-ree-ahnss

expert (n)
un expert
ek-spair
une experte
ek-spairt

explorer (n)
un explorateur
ek-splor-a-tuhr
une exploratrice
ek-splor-a-treess

explosion (n)
une explosion
ek-sploh-zyo(n)

extinct (adj)
éteint (m)
ay-ta(n)
éteinte (f)
ay-tant

extra (adj)
supplémentaire
soo-play-mahn-tair

extremely (adv)
extrêmement
ek-streh-muh-mah(n)

eye (n)
un œil
uh-ye

eyebrow (n)
un sourcil
soor-seel

eyelash (n)
un cil
seel

F

fabulous (adj)
fabuleux (m)
fa-bew-luh
fabuleuse (f)
fa-bew-luhz

face (n)
le visage
vee-zazh

fact (n)
un fait
fay

factory (n)
une usine
ew-zeen

faint (pale) (adj)
faible
fay-bluh

fair (n)
une foire
fwahr

fall (n)
l'automne (m)
loh-ton

false (adj)
faux (m) fausse (f)
foh/fohss

family (n)
une famille
fa-mee-ye

famous (adj)
célèbre
say-lay-bruh

fantastic (adj)
fantastique
fan-tas-teek

far (adv)
loin
lwa(n)

farm (n)
une ferme
fairm

farmer (n)
un fermier
fairm-yay
une fermière
fairm-yair

fashion (n)
la mode
mod

fashionable (adj)
à la mode
ah la mod

fast (adv)
rapide
rap-eed

fat (adj)
gros (m) grosse (f)
groh/grohss

father (n)
un père
pair

faucet (n)
un robinet
ro-bee-nay

favorite (adj)
préféré (m)
préférée (f)
pray-fair-ay

feast (n)
un banquet
bahn-kay

feather (n)
une plume
plewm

felt-tip pen (n)
un feutre
fuh-truh

female (human) (n)
une femme
fam

fence (n)
une barrière
bar-yair

ferry (n)
un ferry
fay-ree

festival (n)
une fête
feht

field (n)
un champ
shah(m)

fierce (adj)
féroce
fair-os

film (n)
un film
feelm

fin (n)
une nageoire
nazh-wahr

fine (adv)
bien
bya(n)

finger (n)
un doigt
dwa

fingernail (n)
un ongle
ong-luh

fingerprint (n)
une empreinte
ahm-prant

fire (n)
le feu
fuh

fire engine (n)
un camion de
pompier
kam-yo(n) duh pomp-yay

firefighter (n)
un pompier
pomp-yay
une femme pompier
fam pomp-yay

firework (n)
un feu d'artifice
fuh dar-tee-feess

first (adv)
d'abord
da-bor

first (adj)
premier (m)
pruhm-yay
première (f)
pruhm-yair

first aid (n)
les premiers secours
pruhm-yay suh-koor

fish (n)
un poisson
pwa-so(n)

fishing (n)
la pêche
pehsh

fishing boat (n)
un bateau de pêche
ba-toh duh pehsh

fit (adj)
en forme
ah(n) form

flag (n)
un drapeau
dra-poh

flame (n)
une flamme
flahm

flashlight (n)
une lampe de poche
lahmp duh posh

flat (adj)
plat (m)
plate (f)
pla/plat

fleece (n)
une polaire
po-lair

flight (n)
un vol
vol

flipper (n)
une palme
palm

flock (of sheep) (n)
un troupeau
troo-poh

flood (n)
une inondation
in-on-da-syo(n)

floor (n)
le sol
sol

flour (n)
la farine
far-een

flower (n)
une fleur
fluhr

flu (n)
la grippe
la greep

flute (n)
une flûte
flewt

fly (n)
une mouche
moosh

fog (n)
le brouillard
broo-yar

A
B
C
D
E
F
G
H
I
J
K
L
M
N
O
P
Q
R
S
T
U
V
W
X
Y
Z
20

food (n)
la nourriture
noo-ree-tewr

foot (human) (n)
le pied
pyay

foot (animal) (n)
une patte
pat

foreign (adj)
étranger (m)
ay-trahn-zhay
étrangère (f)
ay-trahn-zhair

forest (n)
une forêt
fo-reh

fork (n)
une fourchette
foor-shet

forward (adv)
en avant
ah(n) av-ah(n)

fountain (n)
une fontaine
fon-tehn

fox (n)
un renard
ruh-nar

frame (n)
un cadre
kah-druh

freckle (n)
une tache de
rousseur
tash duh roo-suhr

free (adj)
libre
lee-bruh

free time (n)
le temps libre
tah(n) lee-bruh

freedom (n)
la liberté
lee-bair-tay

freezer (n)
un congélateur
kon-zhay-la-tuhr

French (n)
le français
frahn-say

French fries (n)
les frites
freet

fresh (adj)
frais (m)
fraîche (f)
fray/frehsh

friend (n)
un ami, une amie
a-mee

friendly (adj)
amical (m)
amicale (f)
a-mee-kal

frightened (adj)
effrayé (m)
effrayée (f)
eh-fray-yay

frog (n)
une grenouille
gruh-noo-ye

from (prep)
de
duh

front door (n)
une porte d'entrée
port dahn-tray

frosty (weather) (adj)
glacial (m)
glaciale (f)
glass-yal

frozen (adj)
gelé (m) gelée (f)
zhuh-lay

fruit (n)
un fruit
frwee

fruit salad (n)
une salade de
fruits
sal-ad duh frwee

frying pan (n)
une poêle
pwal

fuel (n)
le carburant
kar-bew-rah(n)

full (adj)
plein (m)
pleine (f)
pla(n)/plen

fun (n)
un amusement
am-ewz-mah(n)

fun (adj)
rigolo
ree-go-loh

funny (adj)
drôle
drohl

fur (n)
les poils
pwal

furniture (n)
les meubles
muh-bluh

future (n)
l'avenir (m)
lav-neer

G

galaxy (n)
une galaxie
gal-ak-see

gale (n)
un grand vent
grah(n) vah(n)

game (n)
un jeu
zhuh

game reserve (n)
une réserve
ray-zairv

gang (n)
une bande
bahnd

garage (n)
un garage
gar-azh

garbage (n)
les ordures
or-dewr

garden (n)
un jardin
zhar-da(n)

gardener (n)
un jardinier
zhar-deen-yay
une jardinière
zhar-deen-yair

gardening (n)
le jardinage
zhar-dee-nazh

gas (n)
le gaz
gahz

gasoline (n)
l'essence (f)
le-sahns

gate (n)
une barrière
bar-yair

gentle (adj)
doux (m)
douce (f)
doo/dooss

gently (adv)
doucement
dooss-mah(n)

geography (n)
la géographie
zhay-o-gra-fee

germ (n)
un microbe
meek-rohb

giant (n)
un géant
zhay-ah(n)

gift (n)
un cadeau
ka-doh

giraffe (n)
une girafe
zhee-raf

girl (n)
une fille
fee-ye

girlfriend (n)
une petite amie
puh-teet a-mee

glacier (n)
un glacier
glass-yay

glass (drink) (n)
un verre
vair

glasses (n)
les lunettes
lew-net

globe (n)
un globe
glob

glove (n)
un gant
gah(n)

glue (n)
la colle
kol

goal (n)
un but
bewt

goat (n)
une chèvre
shay-vruh

God (n)
Dieu
dyuh

goggles (n)
les lunettes de
natation
lew-net duh na-ta-syo(n)

gold (n)
l'or (m)
lor

goldfish (n)
un poisson rouge
pwa-so(n) roozh

golf (n)
le golf
golf

good (adj)
bon (m) bonne (f)
bo(n)/bon

gorilla (n)
un gorille
go-ree-ye

government (n)
un gouvernement
goo-vairn-mah(n)

A B C D E F **G** H I J K L M N O P Q R S T U V W X Y Z

21

A
B
C
D
E
F
G
H
I
J
K
L
M
N
O
P
Q
R
S
T
U
V
W
X
Y
Z

grandchildren (n)
les petits-enfants (m)
puh-teez ahn-fah(n)

granddaughter (n)
une petite-fille
puh-teet fee-ye

grandfather (n)
un grand-père
grah(n)-pair

grandmother (n)
une grand-mère
grah(n)-mair

grandparents (n)
les grands-parents
grah(n)-par-ah(n)

grandson (n)
un petit-fils
puh-tee feess

grape (n)
le raisin
ray-za(n)

grass (n)
l'herbe (f)
lairb

grasshopper (n)
une sauterelle
soht-rel

gravity (n)
la pesanteur
puh-xahn-tuhr

gray (adj)
gris (m) grise (f)
gree/greez

great (adj)
formidable
for-mee-da-bluh

green (adj)
vert (m) verte (f)
vair/vairt

greenhouse (n)
une serre
sair

ground (n)
la terre
tair

group (n)
un groupe
groop

guard (n)
un garde
gard

guest (n)
un invité
une invitée
an-vee-tay

guide (n)
un guide
gheed

guidebook (n)
un guide
gheed

guinea pig (n)
un cochon d'Inde
ko-sho(n) dand

guitar (n)
une guitare
ghee-tar

gymnastics (n)
la gymnastique
zheem-nas-teek

H

habit (n)
l'habitude (f)
lab-ee-tewd

habitat (n)
un habitat
a-bee-ta

hair (n)
les cheveux
shuh-vuh

hairbrush (n)
une brosse à
cheveux
bros ah shuh-vuh

hairdresser (n)
un coiffeur
kwa-fuhr
une coiffeuse
kwa-fuhz

hairy (adj)
poilu (m) poilue (f)
pwa-lew

half (n)
une moitié
mwat-yay

hall (n)
un couloir
kool-wahr

hamster (n)
un hamster
am-stair

hand (n)
une main
ma(n)

handbag (n)
un sac à main
sak ah ma(n)

handkerchief (n)
un mouchoir
moosh-wahr

handsome (adj)
beau (m)
boh
belle (f)
bell

hang-glider (n)
un deltaplane
delta-plan

happy (adj)
content (m)
kon-tah(n)
contente (f)
kon-tahnt

harbor (n)
un port
por

hard (adj)
dur (m) dure (f)
dewr

hard drive (n)
un disque dur
deesk dewr

hare (n)
un lièvre
lyeh-vruh

harm (n)
le mal
mal

harvest (n)
une moisson
mwa-so(n)

hat (n)
un chapeau
sha-poh

hawk (n)
un faucon
foh-ko(n)

hay (n)
le foin
fwa(n)

he (pron)
il
eel

head (n)
une tête
teht

headache (n)
un mal de tête
mal duh teht

headphones (n)
les casques (m)
lay kask

healthy (adj)
en bonne santé
ah(n) bon sahn-tay

heart (n)
un cœur
kuhr

heat (n)
la chaleur
sha-luhr

heavy (adj)
lourd (m) lourde (f)
loor/loord

heel (n)
un talon
tal-o(n)

helicopter (n)
un hélicoptère
ay-lee-kop-tair

helmet (n)
un casque
kask

help (n)
une aide
ehd

her/his (adj)
son (m)
sa (f)
so(n)/sa

her/him (pron)
la (her) le (him)
l' (before a vowel)
la/luh/l

here (adv)
ici
ee-see

hero (n)
un héros
air-o

heron (n)
un héron
air-o(n)

hers/his (pron)
le sien (m)
luh sya(n)
la sienne (f)
la syen

hi
salut
sa-lew

hide-and-seek (n)
cache-cache
kash-kash

high (adj)
haut (m) haute (f)
oh/oht

highway (n)
une autoroute
oh-toh-root

hill (n)
une colline
kol-leen

hip (n)
une hanche
ahnsh

hippopotamus (n)
un hippopotame
eep-o-po-tam

historical (adj)
historique
ee-stor-eek

history (n)
l'histoire (f)
leest-wahr

hive (n)
une ruche
rewsh

hobby (n)
un loisir
lwa-zeer

A
B
C
D
E
F
G
H
I
J
K
L
M
N
O
P
Q
R
S
T
U
V
W
X
Y
Z

hockey (n)
le hockey
ok-ay

hole (n)
un trou
troo

home (n)
la maison
may-zo(n)

homework (n)
les devoirs
duhv-wahr

honey (n)
le miel
myel

hood (n)
une capuche
kap-ewsh

hoof (n)
un sabot
sa-boh

horn (n)
une corne
korn

horrible (adj)
horrible
o-ree-bluh

horse (n)
un cheval
shuh-val

horseback riding (n)
l'équitation (f)
lay-keet-a-syo(n)

hospital (n)
un hôpital
o-pee-tal

hot (adj)
chaud (m)
shoh
chaude (f)
shohd

hot-air balloon (n)
une montgolfière
mohn-golf-yair

hot chocolate (n)
un chocolat chaud
sho-ko-la shoh

hot dog (n)
un hot-dog
ot-dog

hotel (n)
un hôtel
o-tel

hour (n)
l'heure (f)
luhr

house (n)
une maison
may-zo(n)

how (adv)
comment
ko-mah(n)

huge (adj)
énorme
ay-norm

human (n)
un être humain
eh-truh ew-ma(n)

hummingbird (n)
un oiseau-mouche
wa-zoh-moosh

hungry (adj)
affamé (m)
affamée (f)
af-fa-may

hurricane (n)
un ouragan
oo-ra-gah(n)

husband (n)
un mari
ma-ree

hut (n)
une cabane
ka-ban

I

I (pron)
je/j'
zhuh/zh

ice (n)
la glace
glass

ice cream (n)
une glace
glass

ice cube (n)
un glaçon
glass-o(n)

ice hockey (n)
le hockey sur glace
ok-ay soor glass

ice pop (n)
un esquimau
es-kee-moh

ice skating (n)
le patinage sur
glace
pa-tee-nazh soor glass

idea (n)
une idée
ee-day

ill (adj)
malade
ma-lad

illness (n)
une maladie
ma-la-dee

illustration (n)
une illustration
eel-lew-stra-syo(n)

immediately (adv)
tout de suite
too-duh-sweet

important (adj)
important (m)
am-por-tah(n)
importante (f)
am-por-tahnt

impossible (adj)
impossible
am-po-see-bluh

information (n)
une information
an-for-ma-syo(n)

ingredient (n)
un ingrédient
an-gray-diah(n)

injury (n)
une blessure
bless-ewr

ink (n)
l'encre (f)
lahn-kruh

in-line skates (n)
les rollerblades (m)
rollerblades

insect (n)
un insecte
an-sekt

inside (prep)
à l'intérieur de
ah lan-tayr-yuhr duh

instruction (n)
une instruction
an-strewk-syo(n)

instrument (n)
un instrument
an-strew-mah(n)

interesting (adj)
intéressant (m)
an-tair-ay-sah(n)

intéressante (f)
an-tair-ay-sahnt

international (adj)
international (m)
internationale (f)
an-tair-na-syo-nal

Internet (n)
l'Internet (m)
lin-tair-net

into (prep)
dans
dah(n)

introduction (n)
une présentation
pray-zahn-ta-syo(n)

invention (n)
une invention
an-vahn-syo(n)

invisible (adj)
invisible
an-vee-zee-bluh

invitation (n)
une invitation
an-vee-ta-syo(n)

iron (clothes) (n)
un fer à repasser
fair ah ruh-pah-say

island (n)
une île
eel

**IT
(information
technology) (n)**
l'informatique (f)
lan-for-ma-teek

its (adj)
son (m) sa (f)
so(n)/sa

it's (it is)
c'est
say

J

jacket (n)
un blouson
bloo-zo(n)

jam (n)
la confiture
kon-fee-tewr

jaw (n)
une mâchoire
mash-wahr

jeans (n)
un jean
jeen

jellyfish (n)
une méduse
may-dewz

jet (n)
un avion à
réaction
av-yo(n) ah ray-ak-syo(n)

jewel (n)
un bijou
bee-zhoo

jewelry (n)
les bijoux
bee-zhoo

jigsaw puzzle (n)
un puzzle
puh-zluh

job (n)
un emploi
am-plwa

joke (n)
une blague
blag

journey (n)
un voyage
vwa-yazh

A
B
C
D
E
F
G
H
I
J
K
L
M
N
O
P
Q
R
S
T
U
V
W
X
Y
Z

A
B
C
D
E
F
G
H
I
J
K
L
M
N
O
P
Q
R
S
T
U
V
W
X
Y
Z

26

judo (n)
le judo
zhew-doh

juice (n)
le jus
zhew

jump rope (n)
une corde à
sauter
kord ah soh-tay

jungle (n)
la jungle
zhahn-gluh

junk (n)
le bric-à-brac
breek-ah-brak

just (adv)
juste
zhewst

K

kangaroo (n)
un kangourou
kahn-goo-roo

karate (n)
le karaté
ka-ra-tay

kettle (n)
une bouilloire
booy-wahr

key (n)
une clé
klay

keyboard (n)
un clavier
klav-yay

kilogram (n)
un kilogramme
kee-lo-gram

kilometer (n)
un kilomètre
kee-lo-meh-truh

kind (gentle) (adj)
gentil (m)
zhahn-tee
gentille (f)
zhahn-teeye

kind (type) (n)
une sorte
sort

king (n)
un roi
rwa

kiss (n)
un baiser
bay-zay

kitchen (n)
une cuisine
kwee-zeen

kite (n)
un cerf-volant
sair-vo-lah(n)

kitten (n)
un chaton
sha-to(n)

knee (n)
un genou
zhuh-noo

knife (n)
un couteau
koo-toh

knight (n)
un chevalier
shuh-val-yay

knot (n)
un nœud
nuh

knowledge (n)
la connaissance
kon-nehs-sahns

koala (n)
un koala
ko-a-la

L

ladder (n)
une échelle
ay-shell

ladybug (n)
une coccinelle
kok-see-nel

lake (n)
un lac
lak

lamb (n)
un agneau
an-yoh

lamp (n)
une lampe
lahmp

land (n)
un terrain
tair-ra(n)

language (n)
une langue
lahn-guh

laptop (n)
un ordinateur
portable
or-dee-na-tuhr por-ta-bluh

large (adj)
gros (m)
groh
grosse (f)
grohss

laser (n)
un laser
laz-air

last (adj)
dernier (m)
dairn-yay

dernière (f)
dairn-yair

last name (n)
le nom de famille
no(m) duh fa-mee-ye

late (adv)
en retard
ah(n) ruh-tar

law (n)
une loi
lwa

lawn (n)
une pelouse
puh-looz

lawn mower (n)
une tondeuse à
gazon
ton-duhz ah gah-zo(n)

lazy (adj)
paresseux (m)
pa-re-suh
paresseuse (f)
pa-re-suhz

leader (n)
le chef
shef

leaf (n)
une feuille
fuh-ye

leather (adj)
en cuir
ah(n) kweer

left (adj)
gauche
gohsh

left-handed (adj)
gaucher (m)
goh-shay
gauchère (f)
goh-shair

leg (n)
une jambe
zhahmb

legs (animal) (n)
les pattes (f)
pat

lemon (n)
un citron
see-tro(n)

lemonade (n)
une limonade
lee-mon-ad

leopard (n)
un léopard
lay-o-par

lesson (n)
une leçon
le-so(n)

letter (n)
une lettre
let-truh

lettuce (n)
une laitue
lay-tew

level (adj)
plat (m) plate (f)
pla/plat

library (n)
une bibliothèque
bee-blee-yo-tek

lid (n)
un couvercle
koo-vair-kluh

life (n)
la vie
vee

lifeboat (n)
un bateau de
sauvetage
ba-toh duh sohv-tazh

lifeguard (n)
un surveillant de
baignade
*soor-vay-ah(n) duh
bayn-yad*

life jacket (n)
un gilet de
sauvetage
zhee-lay duh sohv-tazh

light (not heavy) (adj)
léger (m) légère (f)
lay-zhay/lay-zhehr

light (pale) (adj)
clair (m) claire (f)
klair

light (n)
une lumière
lewm-yair

lighthouse (n)
un phare
far

lightning (n)
un éclair
ay-klair

like (prep)
comme
kom

line (n)
une ligne
leen-ye

line (of people) (n)
une queue
kuh

lion (n)
un lion
lee-yo(n)

lips (n)
les lèvres (f)
leh-vruh

liquid (n)
un liquide
lee-keed

list (n)
une liste
leest

liter (n)
un litre
lee-truh

little (adj)
petit (m) petite (f)
puh-tee/puh-teet

living room (n)
un salon
sal-o(n)

lizard (n)
un lézard
lay-zar

lock (n)
une serrure
sair-rewr

locomotive (n)
une locomotive
lo-ko-mo-teev

log (wood) (n)
une bûche
bewsh

long (adj)
long (m) longue (f)
lo(n)/lon-guh

loose (adj)
ample
ahm-pluh

lost (adj)
perdu (m) perdue (f)
pair-dew

(a) lot (adj)
beaucoup
boh-koo

loud (adj)
bruyant (m)
brew-yah(n)
bruyante (f)
brew-yahnt

loudspeaker (n)
un haut-parleur
oh par-luhr

lovely (adj)
adorable
a-do-ra-bluh

low (adj)
bas (m) basse (f)
bah/bahss

lucky (adj)
chanceux (m)
shahn-suh
chanceuse (f)
shahn-suhz

luggage (n)
les bagages
bag-azh

lunch (n)
le déjeuner
day-zhuh-nay

lunch box (n)
un panier repas
pan-yay ruh-pah

lungs (n)
les poumons (m)
poo-mo(n)

M

machine (n)
une machine
ma-sheen

magazine (n)
un magazine
ma-ga-zeen

magician (n)
un magicien
ma-zhee-sya(n)
une magicienne
ma-zhee-syen

magnet (n)
un aimant
eh-mah(n)

magnetic (adj)
magnétique
man-yet-eek

magnifying glass (n)
une loupe
loop

mail (n)
la poste
post

mailbox (n)
une boîte aux lettres
bwat oh let-truh

mailman (n)
un facteur
fak-tuhr
une factrice
fak-treess

main (adj)
principal (m)
principale (f)
prahn-see-pal

makeup (n)
le maquillage
ma-kee-yazh

male (human) (n)
un homme
om

mammal (n)
un mammifère
ma-mee-fair

man (n)
un homme
om

map (n)
une carte
kart

marbles (toy) (n)
les billes
bee-ye

mark (n)
une note
noht

market (n)
un marché
mar-shay

marriage (n)
le mariage
mar-yazh

married (adj)
marié (m) mariée (f)
mar-yay

mask (n)
un masque
mask

masquerade (n)
un déguisement
day-gheez-mah(n)

mat (n)
un petit tapis
puh-tee ta-pee

match (soccer) (n)
un match
match

matchbox (n)
une boîte
d'allumettes
bwat dal-lew-met

math (n)
les mathématiques
ma-tay-ma-teek

mattress (n)
un matelas
mat-la

maybe (adv)
peut-être
puht-eh-truh

me (pron)
me/m' (vowel)
muh/m

meal (n)
un repas
ruh-pah

meaning (n)
un sens
sahnss

measles (n)
la rougeole
la roozh-ol

measurement (n)
une mesure
muh-zewr

meat (n)
la viande
vyahnd

medal (n)
une médaille
may-da-ye

medicine (n)
un médicament
may-dee-ka-mah(n)

medium (adj)
moyen (m)
mwa-ya(n)
moyenne (f)
mwa-yen

melon (n)
un melon
muh-lo(n)

memory (n)
la mémoire
may-mwahr

menu (n)
la carte
kart

mess (n)
le désordre
day-zor-druh

message (n)
un message
mess-azh

meter (n)
un mètre
meh-truh

microchip (n)
une puce (f)
poos

microscope (n)
un microscope
mee-kro-skop

microwave (n)
un micro-ondes
mee-kro-ond

middle (n)
le milieu
meel-yuh

midnight (n)
minuit
mee-nwee

milk (n)
le lait
lay

milk shake (n)
un milk-shake
meelk-shayk

million
million
meel-yo(n)

millipede
un mille-pattes (m)
meel-pat

mineral (n)
un minéral
mee-nay-ral

minute (n)
une minute
mee-newt

mirror (n)
un miroir
meer-wahr

A
B
C
D
E
F
G
H
I
J
K
L
M
N
O
P
Q
R
S
T
U
V
W
X
Y
Z

A
B
C
D
E
F
G
H
I
J
K
L
Ⓜ
N
O
P
Q
R
S
T
U
V
W
X
Y
Z

miserable (adj)
malheureux (m)
mal-uhr-uh
malheureuse (f)
mal-uhr-uhz

mistake (n)
une erreur
er-ruhr

misty (adj)
brumeux (m)
brew-muh
brumeuse (f)
brew-muhz

mitten (n)
une mitaine
mee-tehn

mixture (n)
un mélange
may-lahnzh

modeling clay (n)
la pâte à modeler
paht ah mod-lay

moment (n)
un instant (m)
an-stah(n)

money (n)
l'argent (m)
lar-zhah(n)

monkey (n)
un singe
sanzh

monster (n)
un monstre
mon-struh

month (n)
un mois
mwa

moon (n)
la lune
lewn

more than
plus que
plews kuh

morning (n)
le matin
ma-ta(n)

mosque (n)
une mosquée
mos-kay

mosquito (n)
un moustique
moos-teek

moth (n)
un papillon de nuit
pa-pee-yo(n) duh nwee

mother (n)
une mère
mair

motor (n)
un moteur
mo-tuhr

motorcycle (n)
une moto
moh-toh

mountain (n)
une montagne
mon-tan-ye

mountain bike (n)
un V. T. T.
vay-tay-tay

mouse (animal) (n)
une souris
soo-ree

mouse (computer) (n)
une souris
soo-ree

mouse pad (n)
un tapis de souris
ta-pee duh soo-ree

moustache (n)
une moustache
moo-stash

mouth (n)
une bouche
boosh

movie star (n)
une vedette de cinéma
vuh-det duh see-nay-ma

movie theater (n)
un cinéma
see-nay-ma

mud (n)
la boue
boo

muddy (adj)
boueux (m)
boo-uh
boueuse (f)
boo-uhz

mug (n)
une tasse
tahss

mom (n)
maman
mah-mah(n)

muscle (n)
un muscle
mew-skluh

museum (n)
un musée
mew-zay

mushroom (n)
un champignon
shahm-peen-yo(n)

music (n)
la musique
mew-zeek

musician (n)
un musicien
mew-zee-sya(n)
une musicienne
mew-zee-syen

my (adj)
mon (m)
ma (f)
mo(n)/ma

N

nail (n)
un ongle
ong-luh

name (n)
un nom
no(m)

narrow (adj)
étroit (m)
étroite (f)
ay-trwa/ay-trwat

nasty (unkind) (adj)
méchant (m)
may-shah(n)
méchante (f)
may-shahnt

nature (n)
la nature
nat-ewr

naughty (adj)
vilain (m)
vee-la(n)
vilaine (f)
veelehn

near (prep)
près de
preh duh

nearly (adv)
presque
presk

neck (n)
un cou
koo

necklace (n)
un collier
kol-yay

needle (n)
une aiguille
ehg-wee-ye

neighbor (n)
un voisin
vwa-za(n)
une voisine
vwa-zeen

nephew (n)
un neveu
nuh-vuh

nerves (n)
les nerfs (m)
nair

nest (n)
un nid
nee

net (n)
une épuisette
ay-pwee-zet

never (adv)
jamais
zha-may

new (adj)
nouveau (m)
noo-voh
nouvelle (f)
noo-vel

news (n)
les nouvelles
noo-vel

newspaper (n)
un journal
zhoor-nal

next (adj)
prochain (m)
prosh-a(n)
prochaine (f)
prosh-ehn

nice (adj)
sympathique
sam-pa-teek

nickname (n)
un surnom
soor-no(m)

niece (n)
une nièce
nyehs

night (n)
la nuit
nwee

no (adv)
non
no(n)

nobody (pron)
personne
pair-son

noisy (adj)
bruyant (m)
brew-yah(n)
bruyante (f)
brew-yahnt

noodles (n)
les nouilles
noo-ye

north (n)
le nord
nor

nose (n)
un nez
nay

nostril (n)
une narine
nar-een

A
B
C
D
E
F
G
H
I
J
K
L
M
N
O
P
Q
R
S
T
U
V
W
X
Y
Z

note (n)
un billet
bee-yay

notebook (n)
un carnet
kar-nay

nothing (n/pron)
rien
rya(n)

now (adv)
maintenant
mehn-tuh-nah(n)

nowhere (adv)
nulle part
newl par

number (n)
un nombre
nom-bruh

nurse (n)
une infirmière
an-feerm-yair

nursery (n)
une crèche
krehsh

O

oar (n)
une rame
ram

oasis (n)
une oasis
o-az-eess

object (n)
un objet
ob-zhay

ocean (n)
un océan
o-say-ah(n)

octopus (n)
une pieuvre
pyuh-vruh

odd (strange) (adj)
bizarre
bee-zar

office (n)
un bureau
bew-roh

office worker (n)
employé (m) de
bureau
employée (f) de
bureau
ahm-plwa-yay duh bew-roh

often (adv)
souvent
soo-vah(n)

oil (n)
l'huile (f)
lweel

old (adj)
vieux (m)
vieille (f)
vyuh/vyay

old-fashioned (adj)
démodé (m)
démodée (f)
day-mo-day

old person (n)
une personne âgée
pair-son ah-zhay

Olympic Games (n)
les Jeux olympiques
zhuz o-leem-peek

omelette (n)
une omelette
om-let

on foot (adv)
à pied
ah pyay

on top of (prep)
sur
soor

once (adv)
une fois
ewn fwa

onion (n)
un oignon
ohn-yo(n)

only (adv)
seulement
suhl-mah(n)

open (adj)
ouvert (m)
ouverte (f)
oo-vair
oo-vairt

opening hours (n)
les heures
d'ouverture
uhr doo-vair-tewr

operation (n)
une opération
o-pair-a-syo(n)

opposite (n)
un contraire
kon-trair

opposite (prep)
en face de
ah(n) fass duh

or (conj)
ou
oo

orange (color) (adj)
orange
or-ahnzh

orange (fruit) (n)
une orange
or-ahnzh

orange juice (n)
un jus d'orange
zhew dor-ahnzh

orchestra (n)
un orchestre
or-ke-struh

organic (adj)
biologique
byo-lo-zheek

ornament (n)
un bibelot
beeb-loh

ostrich (n)
une autruche
oh-trewsh

other (adj)
autre
oh-truh

ouch!
aïe!
eye-ye

our (adj)
notre (m/f)
no-truh

out of (prep)
hors de
or duh

outside (adv)
dehors
duh-or

oval (n)
un ovale
o-val

oven (n)
un four
foor

oven mitt (n)
un gant de cuisine
gah(n) duh kwee-zeen

over there (adv)
là-bas
la-bah

owl (n)
un hibou
ee-boo

own (adj)
propre
pro-pruh

oxygen (n)
l'oxygène (m)
lok-see-zhen

ozone layer (n)
la couche d'ozone
koosh doh-zohne

P

package (n)
un colis
ko-lee

padlock (n)
un cadenas
kad-na

page (n)
une page
pazh

paint (n)
la peinture
pan-tewr

paint brush (n)
un pinceau
pan-soh

paint can (n)
un pot de peinture
poh duh pan-tewr

pair (n)
une paire
pair

pajamas (n)
un pyjama
pee-zha-ma

pale (adj)
pâle
pahl

palm tree (n)
un palmier
palm-yay

pancake (n)
une crêpe
krehp

panda (n)
un panda
pahn-da

pants (n)
un pantalon
pahn-ta-lo(n)

paper (n)
le papier
pap-yay

paper clip (n)
un trombone
trom-bon

paper towel (n)
un essuie-tout
es-swee too

parachute (n)
un parachute
pa-ra-shewt

parade (n)
un défilé
day-fee-lay

parent (n)
un parent
par-ah(n)

park (n)
un parc
park

parrot (n)
un perroquet
pair-o-kay

A B C D E F G H I J K L M N **O** **P** Q R S T U V W X Y Z

A
B
C
D
E
F
G
H
I
J
K
L
M
N
O
P
Q
R
S
T
U
V
W
X
Y
Z

part (n)
une partie
par-tee

partner (n)
un/une camarade
ka-ma-rad

party (n)
une fête
feht

passenger (n)
un passager
pah-sa-zhay
une passagère
pah-sa-zhair

passport (n)
un passeport
pah-spor

past (history) (n)
le passé
pah-say

past (prep)
après
ap-reh

pasta (n)
les pâtes
paht

path (n)
un chemin
shuh-ma(n)

patient (adj)
patient (m)
pa-sya(n)
patiente (f)
pa-syant

pattern (n)
un motif
mo-teef

paw (n)
une patte
pat

pay (n)
un salaire
sa-lair

PC
(personal computer) (n)
un PC
pay-say

PE
(physical education) (n)
l'éducation
physique (f)
lay-dew-ka-syo(n) fee-zeek

pea (n)
un petit pois
puh-tee pwa

peace (n)
la paix
pay

peaceful (adj)
tranquille
trahn-keel

peanut (n)
une cacahuète
ka-ka-weht

pear (n)
une poire
pwahr

pearl (n)
une perle
pairl

pebble (n)
un galet
ga-lay

pedal (n)
une pédale
pay-dal

pelican (n)
un pélican
pay-lee-kah(n)

pen (n)
un stylo
stee-loh

pencil (n)
un crayon à papier
kray-o(n) ah pap-yay

pencil case (n)
une trousse
trooss

penguin (n)
un pingouin
pa(n)-gwa(n)

people (n)
les gens (pl)
zhah(n)

pepper (n)
le poivre
pwa-vruh

perfect (adj)
parfait (m)
par-fay
parfaite (f)
par-feht

perhaps (adv)
peut-être
puh-teh-truh

person (n)
une personne
pair-son

pet (n)
un animal familier
an-ee-mal fa-meel-yay

pharmacy (n)
une pharmacie
far-ma-see

phone (n)
un téléphone
tay-lay-fon

photo (n)
une photo
fo-toh

piano (n)
un piano
piano

picnic (n)
un pique-nique
peek-neek

picture (n)
une image
ee-mazh

piece (n)
un morceau
mor-soh

pig (n)
un cochon
ko-sho(n)

pillow (n)
un oreiller
o-ray-yay

pilot (n)
un pilote
pee-lot

pineapple (n)
un ananas
an-an-ass

pinecone (n)
une pomme
de pin
pom duh pa(n)

pine tree (n)
un pin
pa(n)

pink (adj)
rose
rohz

pirate (n)
un pirate
pee-rat

pitcher (n)
une cruche
krewsh

pizza (n)
une pizza
peed-za

place (n)
un endroit
ahn-drwa

plan (n)
un plan
plah(n)

plane (n)
un avion
av-yo(n)

planet (n)
une planète
plan-eht

plant (n)
une plante
plahnt

plastic (adj)
en plastique
ah(n) plas-teek

plastic bag (n)
un sac en plastique
sak ah(n) plas-teek

plate (n)
une assiette
a-syet

platform (n)
un quai
kay

play (n)
une pièce de théâtre
pyehs duh tay-a-truh

player (n)
un joueur
zhoo-uhr
une joueuse
zhoo-uhz

playground (n)
une cour de
récréation
koor duh ray-kray-a-syo(n)

playtime (n)
une récréation
ray-kray-a-syo(n)

please (adv)
s'il te plaît/
s'il vous plaît
seel tuh pleh/seel voo pleh

plug (for bathtub) (n)
un bouchon
boo-sho(n)

plug (electric) (n)
une prise
électrique
preez ay-lek-treek

plum (n)
une prune
prewn

pocket (n)
une poche
posh

point (n)
un point
pwa(n)

pointed (adj)
pointu (m)
pointue (f)
pwan-tew

polar bear (n)
un ours blanc
oorss blah(n)

pole (post) (n)
un poteau
po-toh

police (n)
la police
po-leess

police car (n)
une voiture de
police
vwa-tewr duh po-leess

police helicopter (n)
un hélicoptère
de police
ay-lee-kop-tair duh po-leess

A
B
C
D
E
F
G
H
I
J
K
L
M
N
O
P
Q
R
S
T
U
V
W
X
Y
Z

A
B
C
D
E
F
G
H
I
J
K
L
M
N
O
P
Q
R
S
T
U
V
W
X
Y
Z

police officer (n)
un policier
po-lee-syay
une femme policier
fam po-lee-syay

polite (adj)
poli (m) polie (f)
po-lee

pollution (n)
la pollution
pol-lew-syo(n)

pond (n)
un étang
ay-tah(n)

pony (n)
un poney
po-nay

poor (adj)
pauvre
poh-vruh

popular (adj)
populaire
po-pew-lair

population (n)
la population
po-pew-la-syo(n)

port (n)
un port
por

portrait (n)
un portrait
por-tray

position (n)
une position
poh-zee-syo(n)

possible (adj)
possible
po-see-bluh

postcard (n)
une carte postale
kart pos-tal

poster (n)
une affiche
af-feesh

post office (n)
un bureau de poste
bew-roh duh post

potato (n)
une pomme de terre
pom duh tair

potato chips (n)
les chips (f)
sheeps

pottery (n)
une poterie (f)
pot-ree

powder (n)
la poudre
poo-druh

powerful (adj)
puissant (m)
pwee-sah(n)
puissante (f)
pwee-sahnt

practice (n)
la répétition
ray-pay-tee-syo(n)

preparations (n)
les préparatifs (m)
pray-para-teef

present (n)
un cadeau
ka-doh

president (n)
un président
pray-zee-dah(n)

pretty (adj)
joli (m) jolie (f)
zho-lee

prey (n)
la proie
prwa

price (n)
un prix
pree

prince (n)
un prince
pranss

princess (n)
une princesse
pran-sess

printout (n)
une impression
am-preh-syo(n)

private (adj)
privé (m)
privée (f)
pree-vay

prize (n)
un prix
pree

probably (adv)
probablement
pro-bab-luh-mah(n)

problem (n)
un problème
prob-lehm

program (TV) (n)
une émission
ay-mee-syo(n)

project (n)
un projet
pro-zhay

proud (adj)
fier (m)
fyer
fière (f)
fy-air

public (adj)
public (m)
publique (f)
pewb-leek

pudding (n)
un dessert
duh-sair

pumpkin (n)
une citrouille
see-troo-ye

pupil (n)
un/une élève
ay-lehv

puppet (n)
une marionnette
mar-yon-net

puppet show (n)
un spectacle de
marionnettes
*spek-tak-luh duh
mar-yon-net*

puppy (n)
un chiot
shyoh

purple (adj)
violet (m) violette (f)
vyo-lay/vyo-let

puzzle (n)
un puzzle
puh-zluh

pyramid (n)
une pyramide
pee-ra-meed

Q

quantity (n)
une quantité
kahn-tee-tay

quarrel (n)
une dispute
dee-spewt

quarter (n)
un quart
kar

queen (n)
une reine
rehn

question (n)
une question
kest-yo(n)

quickly (adv)
vite
veet

quiet (adj)
silencieux (m)
see-lahn-syuh
silencieuse (f)
see-lahn-syuhz

quietly (adv)
tranquillement
trahn-keel-mah(n)

quiz (n)
un quiz
kweez

R

rabbit (n)
un lapin
lap-a(n)

race (n)
une course
koorss

race car (n)
une voiture de
course
vwa-tewr duh koorss

racket (n)
une raquette
rak-et

radio (n)
une radio
rad-yo

railroad station (n)
une gare
gar

rain (n)
la pluie
plwee

rainbow (n)
un arc-en-ciel
ark-ah(n)-syel

raincoat (n)
un imperméable
am-pair-may-a-bluh

rain forest (n)
la forêt tropicale
for-eh tro-pee-kal

rake (n)
un râteau
rah-toh

ranch (n)
un ranch
rahnch

rare (adj)
rare
rahr

raspberry (n)
une framboise
frahm-bwaz

rat (n)
un rat
ra

raw (adj)
cru (m) crue (f)
krew

reading (n)
la lecture
lek-tewr

ready (adj)
prêt (m)
preh
prête (f)
preht

real (adj)
réel (m)
réelle (f)
ray-el

really (adv)
vraiment
vray-mah(n)

receipt (n)
un ticket de caisse
tee-kay duh kess

recipe (n)
une recette
ruh-set

rectangle (n)
un rectangle
rek-tahn-gluh

red (adj)
rouge
roozh

referee (n)
un arbitre
ar-bee-truh

refrigerator (n)
un réfrigérateur
ray-free-zhair-a-tuhr

religion (n)
la religion
ruh-lee-zhyo(n)

remote control (n)
une télécommande
tay-lay-kom-mahnd

report card (for school) (n)
un exposé
ek-spoh-zay

rescue (n)
les secours
suh-koor

restaurant (n)
un restaurant
res-tor-ah(n)

reward (n)
une récompense
ray-kom-pahns

rhinoceros (n)
un rhinocéros
ree-no-say-ros

ribbon (n)
un ruban
rew-bah(n)

rice (n)
le riz
ree

rich (adj)
riche
reesh

riding (n)
l'équitation (f)
lay-kee-ta-syo(n)

right (not left) (adj)
droit (m)
droite (f)
drwa/drwat

right (correct) (adj)
exact (m)
exacte (f)
eg-zakt

ring (n)
une bague
bag

ripe (adj)
mûr (m) mûre (f)
mewr

river (n)
une rivière
reev-yehr

road (n)
une route
root

robot (n)
un robot
ro-boh

rock (n)
un rocher
ro-shay

rocket (n)
une fusée
few-zay

roll (n)
un petit pain
puh-tee pa(n)

roller skates (n)
les patins à
roulettes (m)
pa-ta-(n) ah roo-let

roof (n)
un toit
twa

room (n)
une pièce
pyehs

root (n)
une racine
ra-seen

rope (n)
une corde
cord

rose (n)
une rose
rohz

rough (adj)
rugueux (m)
rugueuse (f)
rew-ghuh
rew-ghuhz

round (adj)
rond (m) ronde (f)
ro(n)/rond

route (n)
un trajet
tra-zhay

row (line) (n)
une rangée
rahn-zhay

rowboat (n)
un canot
kanoh

A B C D E F G H I J K L M N O P Q **R** S T U V W X Y Z

rubber band (n)
un élastique
ay-la-steek

rucksack (n)
un sac à dos
sak ah doh

rug (n)
un tapis
ta-pee

rugby (n)
le rugby
rewg-bee

ruler (measure) (n)
une règle
reh-gluh

running (n)
la course à pied
koorss ah pyay

runway (n)
une piste
peest

S

sack (n)
un sac
sak

sad (adj)
triste
treest

saddle (n)
une selle
sel

safe (adj)
en sécurité
ah(n) say-kew-ree-tay

sail (n)
une voile
vwal

sailboat (n)
un bateau à voiles
ba-toh ah vwal

sailor (n)
un marin
mar-a(n)

salad (n)
une salade
sal-ad

sales clerk (n)
un vendeur
vahn-duhr
une vendeuse
vahn-duhz

salt (n)
le sel
sel

same (adj)
même
mehm

sand (n)
le sable
sah-bluh

sandal (n)
une sandale
sahn-dal

sandcastle (n)
un château de sable
sha-toh duh sah-bluh

sandwich (n)
un sandwich
sahnd-weetsh

satellite dish (n)
une antenne parabolique
ahn-ten pa-ra-bo-leek

satellite TV (n)
la télévision par satellite
tay-lay-vee-zyo(n) par sa-teh-leet

saucepan (n)
une casserole
kass-rol

sausage (n)
une saucisse
soh-seess

scar (n)
une cicatrice
see-ka-treess

scarf (n)
une écharpe
ay-sharp

school (n)
l'école (f)
lay-kol

school uniform (n)
un uniforme scolaire
ew-nee-form sko-lair

science (n)
les sciences
see-yahnss

scientist (n)
un/une scientifique
see-yahn-tee-feek

scissors (n)
les ciseaux
see-zoh

score (n)
un score
skor

screen (n)
un écran
ay-krah(n)

sea (n)
la mer
mair

seafood (n)
les fruits de mer
frwee duh mair

A B C D E F G H I J K L M N O P Q **R S** T U V W X Y Z

seagull (n)
une mouette
moo-wet

seal (n)
un phoque
fok

sea lion (n)
un lion de mer
lee-yo(n) duh mair

seaside (n)
le bord de la mer
bor duh la mair

season (n)
une saison
seh-zo(n)

seat (n)
un siège
syezh

seat belt (n)
une ceinture de
sécurité
san-tewr duh say-kew-ree-tay

seaweed (n)
une algue
al-guh

second (2nd) (adj)
deuxième
duhz-yehm

second (time) (n)
une seconde
suh-go(n)

secret (n)
un secret
suh-kray

seed (n)
une graine
grehn

semicircle (n)
un demi-cercle
duh-mee sair-kluh

shadow (n)
une ombre
om-bruh

shallow (adj)
peu profond (m)
puh pro-fo(n)
peu profonde (f)
puh pro-fond

shampoo (n)
un shampooing
shahm-pwa(n)

shape (n)
une forme
form

shark (n)
un requin
ruh-ka(n)

sharp (adj)
aigu (m)
aiguë (f)
ehg-ew

she (pron)
elle
el

sheep (n)
un mouton
moo-to(n)

sheepdog (n)
un chien de berger
shya(n) duh bair-zhay

sheet (for bed) (n)
un drap
dra

shelf (n)
une étagère
ay-ta-zhehr

shell (n)
un coquillage
ko-kee-yazh

shiny (adj)
brillant (m)
bree-yah(n)
brillante (f)
bree-yahnt

ship (n)
un navire
na-veer

shirt (n)
une chemise
shuh-meez

shoe (n)
une chaussure
shoh-soor

shopper (n)
un acheteur
ash-tuhr
une acheteuse
ash-tuhz

shopping (n)
les courses
koorss

shopping bag (n)
un sac
sak

shopping list (n)
une liste de
courses
leest duh koorss

short (adj)
court (m)
courte (f)
koor/koort

shorts (n)
un short
short

shoulder (n)
une épaule
ay-pohl

shovel (n)
une pelle
pel

A B C D E F G H I J K L M N O P Q R **S** T U V W X Y Z

show (n)
un spectacle
spek-ta-kluh

shower (n)
une douche
doosh

shrimp (n)
une crevette
kruh-vet

shy (adj)
timide
tee-meed

sick (adj)
malade
ma-lad

sidewalk (n)
un trottoir
trot-wahr

sign (n)
un panneau
pan-noh

silence (n)
le silence (m)
luh see-lahns

silly (adj)
bête
beht

silver (n)
l'argent
lar-zhah(n)

simple (adj)
simple
sam-pluh

since (prep)
depuis
duh-pwee

singing (n)
le chant
shah(n)

sink (n)
un évier
ayv-yay

sister (n)
une sœur
suhr

size (n)
la taille
tah-ye

skate (n)
un roller
ro-lair

skateboard (n)
un skate-board
skate-board

skeleton (n)
un squelette
skuh-let

skiing (n)
le ski
skee

skin (n)
la peau
poh

skirt (n)
une jupe
zhewp

skull (n)
un crâne
kran

sky (n)
le ciel
syel

skyscraper (n)
un gratte-ciel
grat-syel

sled (n)
une luge
lewzh

sleeping bag (n)
un sac de couchage
sak duh koosh-azh

sleeve (n)
une manche
mahnsh

sleigh (n)
un traîneau
treh-noh

slipper (n)
une pantoufle
pahn-too-fluh

slippery (adj)
glissant (m)
glee-sah(n)
glissante (f)
glee-sahnt

slow (adj)
lent (m) lente (f)
lah(n)/lahnt

slowly (adv)
lentement
lahn-tuh-mah(n)

slug (n)
une limace
lee-mass

small (adj)
petit (m) petite (f)
puh-tee/puh-teet

smell (n)
une odeur
o-duhr

smile (n)
un sourire
soo-reer

smoke (n)
la fumée
few-may

smooth (adj)
lisse
leess

snail (n)
un escargot
es-kar-goh

snake (n)
un serpent
sair-pah(n)

sneakers (n)
les baskets
bas-ket

snow (n)
la neige
nehzh

snowball (n)
une boule de neige
bool duh nehzh

snowboard (n)
un snow-board
snow-board

snowflake (n)
un flocon de neige
flo-ko(n) duh nehzh

snowman (n)
un bonhomme
de neige
bon-om duh nehzh

soap (n)
le savon
sa-vo(n)

soccer (game) (n)
le football
foot-bohl

soccer ball (ball) (n)
un ballon de
football
ba-lo(n) duh foot-bohl

sock (n)
une chaussette
shoh-set

sofa (n)
un canapé
ka-na-pay

soft (adj)
doux (m) douce (f)
doo/dooss

soil (n)
la terre
tair

soldier (n)
un soldat (m)
sol-da
une femme soldat (f)
fam sol-da

solid (n)
un solide
sol-eed

some (adj)
quelques
kel-kuh

someone (pron)
quelqu'un
kel-ka(n)

something (pron)
quelque chose
kel-kuh shohz

sometimes (adv)
quelquefois
kel-kuh fwa

somewhere (adv)
quelque part
kel-kuh par

son (n)
un fils
feess

song (n)
une chanson
shahn-so(n)

soon (adv)
bientôt
byan-toh

sound (noise) (n)
un son
so(n)

soup (n)
la soupe
la soop

sour (adj)
acide
ass-eed

south (n)
le sud
sood

souvenir (n)
un souvenir
soov-neer

space (n)
l'espace (m)
less-pass

space rocket (n)
une fusée
few-zay

spaghetti (n)
les spaghettis
spa-get-ee

Spanish (n)
l'espagnol (m)
le-span-yol

special (adj)
particulier (m)
par-tee-kewl-yay
particulière (f)
par-tee-kewl-yair

speech (n)
un discours
dee-skoor

speed (n)
la vitesse
vee-tess

spider (n)
une araignée
ar-ehn-yay

sponge (n)
une éponge
ay-ponzh

spoon (n)
une cuillère
kwee-yehr

sport (n)
un sport
spor

spots (n)
les taches
tash

spring (season) (n)
le printemps
pran-tah(m)

spy (n)
un espion
es-pyo(n)
une espionne
es-pyon

square (n)
un carré
kar-ray

squirrel (n)
un écureuil
ay-kew-ruh-ye

stadium (n)
un stade
stad

stage (theater) (n)
la scène
sehn

stairs (n)
un escalier
es-kal-yay

stamp (n)
un timbre
tam-bruh

star (n)
une étoile
ay-twal

starfish (n)
une étoile de mer
ay-twal duh mair

station (n)
une gare
gar

steak (n)
le steak
stek

steam (n)
la buée
bway

steep (adj)
raide
rehd

stem (n)
une tige
teezh

step (n)
un pas
pa

stepfather (n)
un beau-père
boh-pair

stepmother (n)
une belle-mère
bel-mair

stick (n)
un bâton
bah-to(n)

sticker (n)
un autocollant
oh-to-ko-lah(n)

sticky (adj)
collant (m)
ko-lah(n)
collante (f)
ko-lahnt

still (adj)
immobile
im-mob-eel

stocking (n)
un bas
bah

stomach (n)
un estomac
es-to-ma

stone (n)
une pierre
pyair

stormy (adj)
orageux (m)
or-azh-uh
orageuse (f)
or-azh-uhz

store (n)
un magasin
ma-ga-za(n)

story (tale) (n)
une histoire
eest-wahr

story (floor) (n)
un étage
ay-tazh

stove (n)
une cuisinière
kwee-zeen-yair

straight (adj)
droit (m) droite (f)
drwa/drwat

straight (hair) (adj)
raide
rehd

strange (adj)
étrange
ay-trahnzh

straw (n)
la paille
pah-ye

straw (drinking) (n)
une paille
pah-ye

strawberry (n)
une fraise
frehz

A
B
C
D
E
F
G
H
I
J
K
L
M
N
O
P
Q
R
S
T
U
V
W
X
Y
Z

stream (n)
un ruisseau
rwee-soh

street (n)
une rue
rew

street light (n)
un réverbère
ray-vair-bair

strict (adj)
sévère
say-vehr

string (n)
une ficelle
fee-sel

stripes (n)
les rayures
ray-ewr

strong (adj)
fort (m)
forte (f)
for/fort

student (n)
un/une élève
ay-lehv

studio (n)
un studio
stew-dyoh

stupid (adj)
stupide
stoo-peed

stylish (adj)
élégant (m)
ay-lay-gah(n)
élégante (f)
ay-lay-gahnt

subject (n)
un sujet
soo-zhay

submarine (n)
un sous-marin
soo-ma-ra(n)

**subway
(underground) (n)**
un métro
may-troh

suddenly (adv)
tout à coup
toot ah koo

sugar (n)
le sucre
soo-kruh

suit (n)
un costume
kos-tewm

suitcase (n)
une valise
val-eez

summer (n)
l'été (m)
lay-tay

sun (n)
le soleil
so-laye

sunflower (n)
un tournesol
toor-nuh-sol

sunglasses (n)
les lunettes
de soleil
lew-net duh so-laye

sun hat (n)
un chapeau
sha-poh

sunny (adj)
ensoleillé (m)
ensoleillée (f)
ahn-so-lay-yay

sunrise (n)
le lever de soleil
luh-vay duh so-laye

sun screen (n)
la crème solaire
krehm so-lair

sunset (n)
le coucher de soleil
koo-shay duh so-laye

supermarket (n)
un supermarché
soo-pair-mar-shay

sure (adj)
sûr (m) sûre (f)
soor

surface (n)
une surface
soor-fass

surfboard (n)
une planche de surf
plahnsh duh surf

surfing (n)
le surf
surf

surprise (n)
une surprise
soor-preez

surprising (adj)
étonnant (m)
ay-ton-nah(n)
étonnante (f)
ay-ton-nahnt

swan (n)
un cygne
seen-ye

sweater (n)
un pull
pewl

sweatshirt (n)
un sweat-shirt
swet-shurt

sweet (n)
un bonbon
bo(n)-bo(n)

swimming (n)
la natation
na-ta-syo(n)

swimming pool (n)
une piscine
pee-seen

swimsuit (n)
un maillot de bain
ma-yoh duh ba(n)

swing (n)
une balançoire
ba-lahn-swahr

T

table (n)
une table
tab-luh

table tennis (n)
le tennis de table
ten-neess duh tab-luh

tadpole (n)
un têtard
teh-tar

tail (n)
une queue
kuh

tall (adj)
grand (m)
grah(n)
grande (f)
grahnd

tape measure (n)
un mètre
meh-truh

taxi (n)
un taxi
tak-see

tea (n)
le thé
tay

teacher (n)
un maître (m)
meh-truh
une maîtresse (f)
meh-tress

team (n)
une équipe
ay-keep

teddy bear (n)
un ours en peluche
oorss ah(n) puh-lewsh

teenager (n)
un adolescent (m)
une adolescente (f)
ado-less-ah(n)/ado-less-ahnt

telescope (n)
un télescope
tay-leh-skop

television (n)
une télévision
tay-lay-vee-zyo(n)

temperature (n)
la température
tahm-pair-a-tewr

tennis (n)
le tennis
ten-neess

tent (n)
une tente
tahnt

term (n)
un mot
moh

terrible (adj)
terrible
tair-ee-bluh

test (n)
un contrôle
kon-trohl

text message (n)
un texto
teks-toh

that one (pron)
celui-là
suhl-wee-la

the (article)
le (m) la (f)
l'(vowel)
luh/la/l

theater (n)
le théâtre
tay-a-truh

their (adj)
leur (m/f)
luhr

then (conj)
alors
al-or

there (adv)
là
la

thermometer (n)
un thermomètre
tair-mo-meh-truh

they (pron)
ils (m) elles (f)
eel/el

thick (adj)
épais (m)
épaisse (f)
ay-pay/ay-pehss

thin (adj)
fin (m) fine (f)
fa(n)/feen

thin (slim) (adj)
mince
manss

thing (n)
une chose
shohz

third (adj)
troisième
trwaz-yehm

A B C D E F G H I J K L M N O P Q R S T U V W X Y Z

A
B
C
D
E
F
G
H
I
J
K
L
M
N
O
P
Q
R
S
T
U
V
W
X
Y
Z

thirsty (adj)
assoiffé (m)
assoiffée (f)
a-swa-fay

this one (pron)
celui-ci
suhl-wee-see

thought (n)
une pensée
pahn-say

thousand
mille
meel

throat (n)
la gorge
gorzh

throne (n)
un trône
trohn

through (prep)
à travers
ah tra-vair

thumb (n)
un pouce
pooss

thumbtack (n)
une punaise
pew-nehz

thunderstorm (n)
un orage
or-azh

ticket (n)
un billet
bee-yay

tide (n)
la marée
ma-ray

tie (n)
une cravate
kra-vat

tiger (n)
un tigre
tee-gruh

tight (adj)
serré (m) serrée (f)
sair-ray

tights (n)
les collants
ko-lah(n)

time (n)
l'heure (f)
luhr

timetable (n)
un horaire
or-air

tiny (adj)
minuscule
mee-new-skewl

tired (adj)
fatigué (m)
fatiguée (f)
fa-tee-gay

tissues (n)
les mouchoirs en
papier
moosh-wahrs ah(n) pap-yay

toad (n)
un crapaud
kra-poh

toaster (n)
un grille-pain
gree-ye-pa(n)

today (adv)
aujourd'hui
oh-zhoor-dwee

toe (n)
un orteil
or-teye

together (adv)
ensemble
ahn-sahm-bluh

toilet (n)
les toilettes
twa-let

toilet paper (n)
le papier toilette
pap-yay twa-let

tomato (n)
une tomate
tom-at

tomorrow (adv)
demain
duh-ma(n)

tongue (n)
une langue
lahn-guh

tonight (adv)
cette nuit
set nwee

too (adv)
aussi
oh-see

tool (n)
un outil
oo-tee

tooth (n)
une dent
dah(n)

toothbrush (n)
une brosse à dents
bros ah dah(n)

toothpaste (n)
le dentifrice
dahn-tee-freess

top (n)
le haut
oh

tornado (n)
une tornade
tor-nad

tortoise (n)
une tortue
tor-tew

toucan (n)
un toucan
too-kah(n)

tough (adj)
dur (m)
dure (f)
dewr

tourist (n)
un/une touriste
too-reest

toward (prep)
vers
vair

towel (n)
une serviette
sair-vee-et

town (n)
une ville
veel

toy (n)
un jouet
zhoo-way

toy box (n)
un coffre à
jouets
kof-fruh ah zhoo-way

tracksuit (n)
un survêtement
soor-veht-mah(n)

tractor (n)
un tracteur
trak-tuhr

traffic (n)
la circulation
seer-kew-lah-syo(n)

traffic circle (n)
un tourniquet
toor-nee-kay

traffic lights (n)
les feux de
signalisation
fuh duh seen-ya-lee-za-syo(n)

train (n)
un train
tra(n)

train set (toy) (n)
un train
tra(n)

trampoline (n)
un trampoline
trahm-po-leen

transportation (n)
le transport
trahn-spor

tray (n)
un plateau
pla-toh

tree (n)
un arbre
ar-bruh

triangle (n)
un triangle
tree-yahn-gluh

trip (n)
un voyage
vwa-yazh

tropical (adj)
tropical (m)
tropicale (f)
tro-pee-kal

trouble (n)
un ennui
ahn-wee

trowel (n)
un déplantoir
day-plahnt-wahr

truck (n)
un camion
kam-yo(n)

true (adj)
vrai (m)
vraie (f)
vray

trunk (animal) (n)
une trompe
tromp

trunk (tree) (n)
un tronc
tro(n)

trunks (n)
un maillot de bain
ma-yoh duh ba(n)

truth (n)
la vérité
vay-ree-tay

T-shirt (n)
un tee-shirt
tee-shirt

tube (n)
un tube
tewb

tummy (n)
un ventre
vahn-truh

tune (n)
un air
air

tunnel (n)
un tunnel
tew-nel

turkey (n)
un dindon
dan-do(n)

turn (bend) (n)
un tournant
toor-nah(n)

turtle (n)
une tortue de mer
tor-tew duh mair

twice (adv)
deux fois
duh fwa

A
B
C
D
E
F
G
H
I
J
K
L
M
N
O
P
Q
R
S
T
U
V
W
X
Y
Z

twin (n)
un jumeau
zhew-moh
une jumelle
zhew-mel

tire (n)
un pneu
p-nuh

U

ugly (adj)
laid (m) laide (f)
lay/lehd

umbrella (rain) (n)
un parapluie
pa-ra-plwee

umbrella (sun) (n)
un parasol
pa-ra-sol

uncle (n)
un oncle
onk-luh

uncomfortable (adj)
inconfortable
an-kon-for-ta-bluh

under (prep)
sous
soo

underneath (prep)
au-dessous de
oh duh-soo duh

underwear (n)
les sous-vêtements
soo-veht-mah(n)

unfair (adj)
injuste
an-zhewst

uniform (n)
un uniforme
ew-nee-form

universe (n)
l'univers
lew-nee-vair

university (n)
l'université (f)
lew-nee-vair-see-tay

until (prep)
jusqu'à
zhew-ska

unusual (adj)
inhabituel (m)
inhabituelle (f)
een-ab-ee-tew-el

upside down (adv)
à l'envers
ah lahn-vair

upstairs (adv)
en haut
ah(n) oh

useful (adj)
utile
ew-teel

usually (adv)
d'habitude
da-bee-tewd

V

vacation (n)
les vacances
vak-ahnss

vacuum cleaner (n)
un aspirateur
ass-peer-a-tuhr

valley (n)
une vallée
va-lay

van (n)
une camionnette
kam-yon-net

vegetable (n)
un légume
lay-gewm

vegetarian (n)
un végétarien
vay-zhay-ta-rya(n)
une végétarienne
vay-zhay-ta-ryen

verb (n)
un verbe
vairb

very (adv)
très
treh

vet (n)
un/une vétérinaire
vay-tair-ee-nair

video game (n)
un jeu vidéo
zhuh vee-day-oh

video player (n)
un magnétoscope
man-yay-to-skop

village (n)
un village
vee-lazh

violin (n)
un violon
vyo-lo(n)

virtual reality (n)
la réalité
virtuelle
ray-a-lee-tay
veer-tew-ell

vocabulary (n)
le vocabulaire
vo-ka-bew-lair

voice (n)
la voix
vwa

vulture (n)
un vautour
voh-toor

W

waist (n)
la taille
tah-ye

waiter (n)
un garçon de café
gar-so(n) duh ka-fay

waitress (n)
une serveuse
sair-vuhz

walk (n)
une promenade
pro-muh-nad

wall (n)
un mur
mewr

wallet (n)
un portefeuille
por-tuh-fuh-ye

war (n)
une guerre
gair

wardrobe (n)
une armoire
arm-wahr

warm (adj)
chaud (m)
chaude (f)
shoh/shohd

warning (n)
un avertissement
av-air-tee-smah(n)

washbasin (n)
un lavabo
la-va-boh

washcloth (n)
une serviette de
toilette
sair-vee-et duh twa-let

washing machine (n)
une machine
à laver
ma-sheen ah la-vay

wasp (n)
une guêpe
gehp

watch (n)
une montre
mon-truh

water (n)
l'eau (f)
loh

watering can (n)
un arrosoir
ar-rohz-wahr

water lily (n)
un nénuphar
nay-new-far

watermelon (n)
une pastèque
pas-tehk

waterproof (adj)
imperméable
am-pair-may-a-bluh

wave (n)
une vague
vag

wavy (hair) (adj)
bouclé (m)
bouclée (f)
boo-klay

way in (n)
l'entrée (f)
lahn-tray

way out (n)
la sortie
sor-tee

we (pron)
nous
noo

weak (adj)
faible
fay-bluh

weather (n)
le temps
tah(n)

website (n)
un site web
seet web

weed (n)
une mauvaise
herbe
moh-vayz airb

week (n)
une semaine
suh-mehn

weekend (n)
un week-end
week-end

weight (n)
le poids
pwa

welcome (adj)
bienvenu (m)
bienvenue (f)
byan-vuh-new

well (adv)
bien
bya(n)

west (n)
l'ouest (m)
lwest

wet (adj)
mouillé (m)
mouillée (f)
moo-yay

whale (n)
une baleine
ba-len

wheat (n)
le blé
blay

wheel (n)
une roue
roo

wheelbarrow (n)
une brouette
broo-et

wheelchair (n)
un fauteuil
roulant
foh-tuh-ye roo-lah(n)

when (adv)
quand
kah(n)

where (adv)
où
oo

while (conj)
pendant que
pahn-dah(n) kuh

whisker (n)
une moustache
moo-stash

whistle (n)
un sifflement
see-fluh-mah(n)

white (adj)
blanc (m) blanche (f)
blah(n)/blahnsh

who (pron)
qui
kee

why (adv)
pourquoi
poor-kwa

wide (adj)
large
larzh

wife (n)
une épouse
ay-pooz

wig (n)
une perruque
pair-ewk

wind (n)
le vent
vah(n)

window (n)
une fenêtre
fuh-neh-truh

windy (adj)
il y a du vent
eel ya dew vah(n)

wing (n)
une aile
ehl

winner (n)
un gagnant
gan-yah(n)
une gagnante
gan-yahnt

winter (n)
l'hiver (m)
lee-vair

wise (adj)
sage
sazh

wish (n)
un souhait
sway

with (prep)
avec
av-ek

without (prep)
sans
sah(n)

wolf (n)
un loup
loo

woman (n)
une femme
fam

wood (n)
le bois
bwa

wooden (adj)
en bois
ah(n) bwa

workbook (n)
un cahier
ka-yay

wool (n)
la laine
lehn

woolen hat (n)
un bonnet
bon-nay

word (n)
un mot
moh

work (n)
le travail
tra-vye

world (n)
un monde
mond

worm (n)
un ver
vair

worst (adj)
pire
peer

wound (n)
une blessure
bless-ewr

wrist (n)
un poignet
pwan-ye

writing (act of) (n)
l'écriture (f)
lay-kree-tewr

A B C D E F G H I J K L M N O P Q R S T U V W X Y Z

X

x-ray (n)
une radiographie
rad-yo-gra-fee

Y

yes (adv)
oui
wee

Z

zebra (n)
un zèbre
zeh-bruh

zero (n)
zéro
zay-roh

zip code (n)
un code postal
kohd pos-tal

zipper (n)
une fermeture
éclair
fair-muh-tewr ay-klair

zone (n)
une zone
zohn

zoo (n)
un zoo
zoh

Speaking French

In this dictionary, we have spelled out each French word in a way that will help you pronounce it. Use this guide to help you understand how the word should sound when you say it. Some French words look the same as English, but sound very different!

Letter	Pronunciation	Our spelling	Example
a, à, â	between the *a* in h*a*t and f*a*r	a or ah	**adresse** *a-dreys*
ch	like *sh* in *sh*ip	sh	**changer** *shahn-zhay*
ç	like *s* in *s*it	s	**garçon** *gar-so(n)*
é	like *ay* in d*ay*	ay	**café** *ka-fay*
è, ê	like *e* in m*e*t	eh	**crème** *krehm*
e	like *er* in oth*er*	uh	**de** *duh*
gn	like the *ni* in o*ni*on	nye	**ligne** *leen-ye*
i, y	like *ee* in f*ee*t	ee	**fille** *fee-ye*
j, and sometimes g	like *s* in mea*s*ure	zh	**bonjour** *bon-zhoor*
qu	like *k* in *k*ing	k	**queue** *kuh*
o, ô	like *o* in m*o*re	o or oh	**porte** *port*
r	say *ruh* at the back of your throat, as if you're gargling	r	**fleur** *fluhr*
u	like *ew* in f*ew*	ew	**tu** *tew*
an, en, ien, in, ain, ein, on, un, am, em, im, aim, eim, om, um	the *n* is not pronounced, but the vowel in front of it should have a nasal sound, as if the word ended in *ng*. For example, as if you said *song*, but stopped before saying the final *ng*.	a(n), ah(n), o(n)	**bien** *bya(n)*

A
B
C
D
E
F
G
H
I
J
K
L
M
N
O
P
Q
R
S
T
U
V
W
X
Y
Z

French A–Z

In this section, the French words are given in alphabetical order. They are followed by the English translation and a few letters to show what type of word it is—a noun (n) or adjective (adj), for example. Look at p. 4 to see a list of the different types of words.

Nouns in French are either masculine or feminine. We have used the abbreviations (m) and (f) to tell you which they are. Sometimes a word in French might mean more than one thing in English, so there might be two translations underneath.

Most of the nouns (naming words) here are singular (only one of the object). To make a noun plural (for more than one thing) you usually just add an "s"—the same as in English. In French though, the other words in the sentence change too—**le** and **la** become **les**. The adjectives also change, usually getting an extra "s" at the end.

A

à côté de (prep)
beside

à l'arrière (adv)
back (opposite of front)

à l'envers (adv)
upside down

à l'intérieur de (prep)
inside

à la mode (adv)
fashionable

à pied (adv)
on foot

à travers (prep)
through

abeille (n) (f)
bee

abricot (n) (m)
apricot

absent/absente (adj)
away

accident (n) (m)
accident

acheteur/acheteuse (n) (m/f)
shopper

acide (adj)
sour

activité (n) (f)
activity

acrobate (n) (m/f)
acrobat

acteur (n) (m)
actor

action (n) (f)
action

actrice (n) (f)
actress

addition (n) (f)
bill

adolescent/adolescente (n) (m/f)
teenager

adorable (adj)
lovely

adresse (n) (f)
address

adresse électronique (n) (f)
email address

adulte (n) (m/f)
adult

aéroport (n) (m)
airport

affaires (n) (f)
business

affamé/affamée (adj)
hungry

affiche (n) (f)
poster

âge (n) (m)
age

agneau (n) (m)
lamb

aide (n) (f)
help

aïe!
ouch!

aigle (n) (m)
eagle

Sidebar letters: A B C D E F G H I J K L M N O P Q R S T U V W X Y Z

aigu/aiguë (adj)
sharp

aiguille (n) (f)
needle

aile (n) (f)
wing

aimant (n) (m)
magnet

air (n) (m)
air

air (n) (m)
tune

algue (n) (f)
seaweed

alligator (n) (m)
alligator

alors (conj)
then

alphabet (n) (m)
alphabet

ambulance (n) (f)
ambulance

amer/amère (adj)
bitter

ami/amie (n) (m/f)
friend

amical/amicale (adj)
friendly

ample (adj)
loose

ampoule (n) (f)
bulb (light)

amusement (n) (m)
fun

ananas (n) (m)
pineapple

ancre (n) (f)
anchor

anglais (n) (m)
English

animal (n) (m)
animal

animal familier (n) (m)
pet

année/an (n) (f/m)
year

anniversaire (n) (m)
birthday

antenne (n) (f)
antenna

antenne parabolique (n) (f)
satellite dish

appareil photo (n) (m)
camera

apparence (n) (f)
appearance

appartement (n) (m)
apartment

après (prep)
after, past

après-midi (n) (m)
afternoon

araignée (n) (f)
spider

arbitre (n) (m)
referee

arbre (n) (m)
tree

arc-en-ciel (n) (m)
rainbow

arche (n) (f)
arch

architecte (n) (m/f)
architect

argent (n) (m)
money, silver

argent de poche (n) (m)
allowance

armée (n) (f)
army

armoire (n) (f)
cupboard (tall)

armoire (n) (f)
wardrobe

arrêt de bus (n) (m)
bus stop

arrivée (n) (f)
arrival

arrosoir (n) (m)
watering can

art (n) (m)
art

artiste (n) (m/f)
artist

ascenseur (n) (m)
elevator

aspirateur (n) (m)
vacuum cleaner

assez (adv)
enough

assiette (n) (f)
plate

assistant/assistante (n) (m/f)
assistant

assoiffé/assoiffée (adj)
thirsty

astronaute (n) (m/f)
astronaut

A
B
C
D
E
F
G
H
I
J
K
L
M
N
O
P
Q
R
S
T
U
V
W
X
Y
Z

A
B
C
D
E
F
G
H
I
J
K
L
M
N
O
P
Q
R
S
T
U
V
W
X
Y
Z

astronome (n) (m/f)
astronomer

athlétisme (n) (m)
athletics

atlas (n) (m)
atlas

aube (n) (f)
dawn

au-dessous de (prep)
below

au-dessus de (prep)
above

aujourd'hui (adv)
today

aussi (adv)
also, too

auteur (n) (m)
author

autobus (n) (m)
bus

autocar (n) (m)
coach

autocollant (n) (m)
sticker

automne (n) (m)
fall

autoroute (n) (f)
motorway

autour (prep)
around

autre (adj)
other

autruche (n) (f)
ostrich

au rez-de-chaussée (adv)
downstairs

avant (prep)
before

avec (prep)
with

avenir (n) (m)
future

aventure (n) (f)
adventure

avertissement (n) (m)
warning

avion (n) (m)
aiplane, plane

avion à réaction (n) (m)
jet

avocat (n) (m)
avocado

B

babouin (n) (m)
baboon

bacon (n) (m)
bacon

badminton (n) (m)
badminton

bagages (n) (m)
luggage

bague (n) (f)
ring

baignoire (n) (f)
bath

baiser (n) (m)
kiss

balai (n) (m)
broom

balançoire (n) (f)
swing

balcon (n) (m)
balcony

baleine (n) (f)
whale

balle (n) (f)
ball

ballon (n) (m)
ball, balloon

ballon de football (n) (m)
soccer (ball)

banane (n) (f)
banana

banc (n) (m)
bench

bande (n) (f)
band

bande (n) (f)
gang

bande dessinée (n) (f)
cartoon (drawing)

banque (n) (f)
bank (money)

banquet (n) (m)
feast

barbe (n) (f)
beard

barbecue (n) (m)
barbecue

barrière (n) (f)
fence, gate

bas/basse (adj)
low

bas (n) (m)
stocking

base-ball (n) (m)
baseball

basket-ball (n) (m)
basketball

baskets (n) (f)
sneakers

bataille (n) (f)
battle

bateau (n) (m)
boat

bateau à voiles (n) (m)
sailboat

bateau de pêche (n) (m)
fishing boat

bateau de sauvetage (n) (m)
lifeboat

bâtiment (n) (m)
building

bâton (n) (m)
stick

batte (n) (f)
bat (sports)

batterie (n) (f)
drum kit

beau/belle (adj)
beautiful, handsome

beaucoup (adv)
(a) lot

beau-père (n) (m)
stepfather

beauté (n) (f)
beauty

bébé (n) (m)
baby

bec (n) (m)
beak

belle-mère (n) (f)
stepmother

bétail (n) (m)
cattle

bête (n) (f)
creature

bête (adj)
silly

beurre (n) (m)
butter

bibelot (n) (m)
ornament

bibliothèque (n) (f)
library

bidon (n) (m)
can

bien (adj)
fine

bien (adv)
well

bien que (conj)
although

bientôt (adv)
soon

bienvenu/bienvenue (adj)
welcome

bijou (n) (m)
jewel

bijoux (n) (m)
jewelry

billes (n) (f)
marbles (toy)

billet (n) (m)
note, ticket

biologique (adj)
organic

biscuit (n) (m)
biscuit

bizarre (adj)
odd (strange)

blague (n) (f)
joke

blanc/blanche (adj)
white

blé (n) (m)
wheat

blessure (n) (f)
injury, wound

bleu (n) (m)
bruise

bleu/bleue (adj)
blue

blond/blonde (adj)
blonde

blouson (n) (m)
jacket

bois (n) (m)
wood

boisson (n) (f)
beverage

boîte (n) (f)
box

boîte aux lettres (n) (f)
mailbox

boîte d'allumettes (n) (f)
matchbox

bol (n) (m)
bowl (cereal)

bon/bonne (adj)
good

bonbon (n) (m)
candy

bondé/bondée (adj)
crowded

A B C D E F G H I J K L M N O P Q R S T U V W X Y Z

55

bonhomme de neige (n) (m)
snowman

bon marché (adj)
cheap

bonnet (n) (m)
woolen hat

bord (n) (m)
edge

bord de la mer (n) (m)
seaside

botte (n) (f)
boot

bouche (n) (f)
mouth

boucherie (n) (f)
butcher's store

bouchon (n) (m)
plug

bouclé/bouclée (adj)
wavy (hair)

boucle d'oreille (n) (f)
earring

boue (n) (f)
mud

bouée (n) (f)
buoy

boueux/boueuse (adj)
muddy

bougie (n) (f)
candle

bouilloire (n) (f)
kettle

boulangerie (n) (f)
bakery

boule de neige (n) (f)
snowball

boussole (n) (f)
compass

bouteille (n) (f)
bottle

bouton (n) (m)
button

bracelet (n) (m)
bracelet

branche (n) (f)
branch

bras (n) (m)
arm

bric-à-brac (n) (m)
junk

brillant/brillante (adj)
bright, shiny

brise (n) (f)
breeze

brosse à cheveux (n) (f)
hairbrush

brosse à dents (n) (f)
toothbrush

brouette (n) (f)
wheelbarrow

brouillard (n) (m)
fog

brumeux/brumeuse (adj)
misty

bruyant/bruyante (adj)
loud, noisy

bûche (n) (f)
log (wood)

buée (n) (f)
steam

buisson (n) (m)
bush

bulbe (n) (m)
bulb (plant)

bulle (n) (f)
bubble

bureau (n) (m)
desk, office

bureau de poste (n) (m)
post office

but (n) (m)
goal

C

c'est
it's (it is)

cabane (n) (f)
hut

cabinet médical (n) (m)
surgery (place)

cadeau (n) (m)
gift

cacahuète (n) (f)
peanut

cache-cache (n) (m)
hide-and-seek

caddie (n) (m)
cart
(supermarket)

cadeau (n) (m)
present

cadenas (n) (m)
padlock

cadre (n) (m)
frame

café (n) (m)
café, coffee

cage (n) (f)
cage

cahier (n) (m)
workbook

caisse (n) (f)
checkout

calculatrice (n) (f)
calculator

calendrier (n) (m)
calendar

calme (adj)
calm

camarade (n) (m/f)
partner

camion (n) (m)
truck

camion de pompier
(n) (m)
fire engine

camionnette (n) (f)
van

campagne (n) (f)
countryside

camping (n) (m)
campsite

canapé (n) (m)
sofa

canard (n) (m)
duck

caneton (n) (m)
duckling

canoë (n) (m)
canoe

canot (n) (m)
rowboat

cape (n) (f)
cloak

capitale (n) (f)
capital

capuche (n) (f)
hood

carburant (n) (m)
fuel

caravane (n) (f)
caravan

carnaval (n) (m)
carnival

carnet (n) (m)
notebook

carotte (n) (f)
carrot

carré (n) (m)
square

carrefour (n) (m)
crossing

cartable (n) (m)
book bag

carte (n) (f)
card, map, menu

carte d'anniversaire
(n) (f)
birthday card

carte postale (n) (f)
postcard

cartes (n) (f)
cards

carton (n) (m)
cardboard

casque (n) (m)
helmet

casques (n) (m)
headphones

casquette (n) (f)
cap

cassé/cassée (adj)
broken

casserole (n) (f)
saucepan

cassette (n) (f)
cassette

catastrophe (n) (f)
disaster

cathédrale (n) (f)
cathedral

cave (n) (f)
cellar

CD (n) (m)
CD

ceinture (n) (f)
belt

ceinture de sécurité
(n) (f)
seat belt

célébration (n) (f)
celebration

célèbre (adj)
famous

celui-ci (pron)
this one

celui-là (pron)
that one

centre (n) (m)
center

cercle (n) (m)
circle

céréale (n) (f)
cereal

cerf-volant (n) (m)
kite

cerise (n) (f)
cherry

A
B
C
D
E
F
G
H
I
J
K
L
M
N
O
P
Q
R
S
T
U
V
W
X
Y
Z

A
B
C
D
E
F
G
H
I
J
K
L
M
N
O
P
Q
R
S
T
U
V
W
X
Y
Z

certain/certaine (adj)
certain

cerveau (n) (m)
brain

cette nuit
tonight

chaîne (n) (f)
chain

chaise (n) (f)
chair

chaise longue (n) (f)
deck chair

chaleur (n) (f)
heat

chambre (n) (f)
bedroom

chameau (n) (m)
camel

champ (n) (m)
field

champignon (n) (m)
mushroom

chance (n) (f)
chance

chanceux/chanceuse (adj)
lucky

changement (n) (m)
change

chance (n) (f)
chance

chanson (n) (f)
song

chant (n) (m)
singing

chapeau (n) (m)
hat, sunhat

chaque (adj)
each

charrette (n) (f)
cart

chat (n) (m)
cat

château (n) (m)
castle

château de sable (n) (m)
sandcastle

chaton (n) (m)
kitten

chaud/chaude (adj)
hot, warm

chaussette (n) (f)
sock

chaussure (n) (f)
shoe

chauve (adj)
bald

chauve-souris (n) (f)
bat (animal)

chef (n) (m/f)
chef

chef (n) (m)
leader

chemin (n) (m)
path

cheminée (n) (f)
chimney

chemise (n) (f)
shirt

chemisier (n) (m)
blouse

chenille (n) (f)
caterpillar

cher/chère (adj)
special,
expensive

cheval (n) (m)
horse

chevalier (n) (m)
knight

cheveux (n) (m)
hair

cheville (n) (f)
ankle

chèvre (n) (f)
goat

chewing-gum (n) (m)
chewing gum

chien (n) (m)
dog

chien de berger (n) (m)
sheepdog

chimpanzé (n) (m)
chimpanzee

chiot (n) (m)
puppy

chirurgie (n) (f)
surgery

chocolat (n) (m)
chocolate

chocolat chaud (n) (m)
hot chocolate

choix (n) (m)
choice

chose (n) (f)
thing

chou (n) (m)
cabbage

chou-fleur (n) (m)
cauliflower

cicatrice (n) (f)
scar

ciel (n) (m)
sky

cil (n) (m)
eyelash

cinéma (n) (m)
movie theater

cintre (n) (m)
coat hanger

circulation (n) (f)
traffic

cirque (n) (m)
circus

ciseaux (n) (m)
scissors

citron (n) (m)
lemon

citrouille (n) (f)
pumpkin

clair/claire (adj)
clear, light

classe (n) (f)
class (school)

clavier (n) (m)
keyboard

clé (n) (f)
key

client/cliente (n) (m/f)
customer

cloche (n) (f)
bell

clown (n) (m)
clown

club (n) (m)
club

coccinelle (n) (f)
ladybug

cochon (n) (m)
pig

cochon d'Inde (n) (m)
guinea pig

code postal (n) (m)
zip code

cœur (n) (m)
heart

coffre à jouets (n) (m)
toybox

coiffeur/coiffeuse (n)
(m/f)
hairdresser

coin (n) (m)
corner

colis (n) (m)
parckage

collant/collante (adj)
sticky

collants (n) (m)
tights

colle (n) (f)
glue

collier (n) (m)
collar, necklace

colline (n) (f)
hill

coloré/colorée (adj)
colorful

comique (n) (m)
comic

commandes (n) (f)
controls

comme (prep)
like

comment (adv)
how

commode (n) (f)
chest of drawers

compétition (n) (f)
competition

concert (n) (m)
concert

concombre (n) (m)
cucumber

confiture (n) (f)
jam

confortable (adj)
comfortable

congélateur (n) (m)
freezer

connaissance (n) (f)
knowledge

content/contente (adj)
happy

continent (n) (m)
continent

contraire (n) (m)
opposite

contre (prep)
against

contrôle (n) (m)
test

conversation (n) (f)
conversation

coquillage (n) (m)
shell

corde (n) (f)
rope

corde à sauter (n) (f)
jump rope

A
B
C
D
E
F
G
H
I
J
K
L
M
N
O
P
Q
R
S
T
U
V
W
X
Y
Z

A
B
C
D
E
F
G
H
I
J
K
L
M
N
O
P
Q
R
S
T
U
V
W
X
Y
Z

corne (n) (f)
horn

corps (n) (m)
body

costume (n) (m)
suit

côte (n) (f)
coast

coton (n) (m)
cotton

cou (n) (m)
neck

couche d'ozone (n) (f)
ozone layer

coucher de soleil (n) (m)
sunset

coude (n) (m)
elbow

couette (n) (f)
comforter

couleur (n) (f)
color

couloir (n) (m)
hall, corridor

cour de récréation (n) (f)
playground

courageux/courageuse (adj)
brave

courbe (adj)
curved

couronne (n) (f)
crown

course (n) (f)
race

course à pied (n) (f)
running

courses (n) (f)
shopping

court/courte (adj)
short

cousin/cousine (n) (m/f)
cousin

coussin (n) (m)
cushion

couteau (n) (m)
knife

couvercle (n) (m)
lid

couverture (n) (f)
blanket

cow-boy (n) (m)
cowboy

crabe (n) (m)
crab

crâne (n) (m)
skull

crapaud (n) (m)
toad

cravate (n) (f)
tie

crayon à papier (n) (m)
pencil

crayon de couleur (n) (m)
colored pencil, crayon

crèche (n) (f)
nursery

crème (n) (f)
cream

crème solaire (n) (f)
sunscreen

crêpe (n) (f)
pancake

crépuscule (n) (m)
dusk

crevette (n) (f)
shrimp

crocodile (n) (m)
crocodile

cruche (n) (f)
pitcher

cru/crue (adj)
raw

cruel/cruelle (adj)
cruel

cube (n) (m)
cube

cubes (n) (m)
blocks

cuillère (n) (f)
spoon

cuisine (n) (f)
kitchen

cuisinière (n) (f)
stove

curieux/curieuse (adj)
curious

cygne (n) (m)
swan

D

d'abord (adv)
first

d'habitude (adv)
usually

daim (n) (m)
deer

danger (n) (m)
danger

dangereux/dangereuse (adj)
dangerous

dans (prep)
into

danseur/danseuse (n) (m/f)
dancer

danseur/ danseuse classique (n) (m/f)
ballet dancer

date (n) (f)
date

dauphin (n) (m)
dolphin

de (prep)
from

de l'autre côté de (prep)
across

dé/dés (n) (m)
dice

débutant/débutante (n) (m/f)
beginner

décoration (n) (f)
decoration

défi (n) (m)
challenge

défilé (n) (m)
parade

déguisement (n) (m)
costume, disguise

dehors (adv)
outside

déjà (adv)
already

déjeuner (n) (m)
lunch

délicieux/délicieuse (adj)
delicious

deltaplane (n) (m)
hang-glider

demain (adv)
tomorrow

demi-cercle (n) (m)
semicircle

démodé/démodée (adj)
old-fashioned

dent (n) (f)
tooth

dentifrice (n) (m)
toothpaste

dentiste (n) (m/f)
dentist

déplantoir (n) (m)
trowel

depuis (prep)
since

dernier/dernière (adj)
last

derrière (prep)
behind

désert (n) (m)
desert

désordre (n) (m)
mess

dessert (n) (m)
dessert, pudding

dessin (n) (m)
art, drawing

dessin animé (n) (m)
cartoon (film)

détective (n) (m)
detective

deux fois
twice

deuxième (adj)
second (2nd)

devant (prep)
ahead, in front of

devoirs (n) (m)
homework

diagramme (n) (m)
diagram

dictionnaire (n) (m)
dictionary

Dieu (n) (m)
God

différent/différente (adj)
different

difficile (adj)
difficult

digital/digitale (adj)
digital

dindon (n) (m)
turkey

dîner (n) (m)
dinner

dinosaure (n) (m)
dinosaur

directement (adv)
directly

direction (n) (f)
direction

discothèque (n) (f)
disco

discours (n) (m)
speech

A
B
C
D
E
F
G
H
I
J
K
L
M
N
O
P
Q
R
S
T
U
V
W
X
Y
Z

dispute (n) (f)
quarrel

disque dur (n) (m)
hard drive

distance (n) (f)
distance

divorcé/divorcée (adj)
divorced

doigt (n) (m)
finger

dôme (n) (m)
dome

dos (n) (m)
back (body)

doucement (adv)
gently

douche (n) (f)
shower

doux/douce (adj)
gentle, soft

dragon (n) (m)
dragon

drap (n) (m)
sheet

drapeau (n) (m)
flag

droit/droite (adj)
straight, right
(not left)

drôle (adj)
funny

dur/dure (adj)
hard, tough

DVD (n) (m)
DVD

E

eau (n) (f)
water

échange (n) (m)
exchange

écharpe (n) (f)
scarf

échecs (n) (m)
chess

échelle (n) (f)
ladder

écho (n) (m)
echo

éclair (n) (m)
lightning

école (n) (f)
school

écran (n) (m)
screen

écriture (n) (f)
writing (act of)

écureuil (n) (m)
squirrel

éducation (n) (f)
education

**éducation physique
(n) (f)**
PE (physical
education)

effet (n) (m)
effect

effrayé/effrayée (adj)
frightened

égal/égale (adj)
equal

église (n) (f)
church

élastique (n) (m)
rubber band

électricité (n) (f)
electricity

électrique (adj)
electrical

élégant/élégante (adj)
stylish

éléphant (n) (m)
elephant

élève (n) (m/f)
pupil, student

elle (pron)
she

elles (pron)
they

e-mail (n) (m)
email

émission (n) (f)
program (TV)

**employé/employée de
bureau (n) (m/f)**
office worker

emploi (n) (m)
job

empreinte (n) (f)
fingerprint

en arrière (adv)
backward

en avant (adv)
forward

en bois
wooden

en bonne santé
healthy

encore (adj)
another

en colère
angry

en cuir
leather

en-dessous de (prep)
underneath

endroit (n) (m)
place

énergie (n) (f)
energy

en espèces
(in) cash

ennemi/ennemie (n) (m/f)
enemy

énorme (adj)
enormous

en face de (prep)
opposite

en forme
fit

en haut (adv)
upstairs

en plastique
plastic

en retard
late

en sécurité
safe

encore (adv)
again

encre (n) (f)
ink

encyclopédie (n) (f)
encyclopedia

endroit (n) (m)
place

enfant/enfants (n) (m/f)
child/children

ennui (n) (m)
trouble

ennuyeux/ennuyeuse (adj)
boring

énorme (adj)
enormous

ensemble (adv)
together

ensoleillé/ensoleillée (adj)
sunny

enthousiaste (adj)
enthusiastic

entre (prep)
among, between

entrée (n) (f)
entrance, way in

enveloppe (n) (f)
envelope

environ (adv)
about

environnement (n) (m)
environment

épais/épaisse (adj)
thick

épaule (n) (f)
shoulder

éponge (n) (f)
sponge

épouse (n) (f)
wife

épuisette (n) (f)
net

équateur (n) (m)
equator

équipage (n) (m)
crew

équipe (n) (f)
team

équitation (n) (f)
horseback riding

erreur (n) (f)
mistake

escalier (n) (m)
stairs

escargot (n) (m)
snail

espace (n) (m)
space

espagnol (n) (m)
Spanish

espion/espionne (n) (m/f)
spy

esquimau (n) (m)
ice pop

essence (n) (f)
gasoline

essuie-tout (n) (m)
paper towel

est (n) (m)
east

estomac (n) (m)
stomach

et (conj)
and

étage (n) (m)
story (floor)

étagère (n) (f)
shelf

A
B
C
D
E
F
G
H
I
J
K
L
M
N
O
P
Q
R
S
T
U
V
W
X
Y
Z

étang (n) (m)
pond

été (n) (m)
summer

éteint/éteinte (adj)
extinct

étoile (n) (f)
star

étoile de mer (n) (f)
starfish

étonnant/étonnante (adj)
surprising

étrange (adj)
strange

étranger/étrangère (adj)
foreign

être humain (n) (m)
human

étroit/étroite (adj)
narrow

événement (n) (m)
event

évier (n) (m)
sink

exact/exacte (adj)
right (correct)

exactement (adv)
exactly

examen (n) (m)
exam

excellent/excellente (adj)
excellent

excité/excitée (adj)
excited

excuse (n) (f)
excuse

exemple (n) (m)
example

exercice (n) (m)
exercise

expédition (n) (f)
expedition

expérience (n) (f)
experiment

expert/experte (n) (m/f)
expert

**explorateur/
exploratrice (n) (m/f)**
explorer

explosion (n) (f)
explosion

exposé (n) (m)
report card

exposition (n) (f)
exhibition

extraterrestre (n) (m/f)
alien

extrêmement (adv)
extremely

F

fabuleux/fabuleuse (adj)
fabulous

facile (adj)
easy

facteur/factrice (n) (m/f)
mailman

faible (adj)
faint (pale), weak

fait (n) (m)
fact

falaise (n) (f)
cliff

famille (n) (f)
family

fantastique (adj)
fantastic

farine (n) (f)
flour

fatigué/fatiguée (adj)
tired

faucon (n) (m)
hawk

fauteuil (n) (m)
armchair

fauteuil roulant (n) (m)
wheelchair

faux/fausse (adj)
false

femme (n) (f)
female (human),
woman

fenêtre (n) (f)
window

fer à repasser (n) (m)
iron (clothes)

ferme (n) (f)
farm

fermé/fermée (adj)
closed

fermeture éclair (n) (f)
zipper

fermier/fermière (n) (m/f)
farmer

féroce (adj)
fierce

ferry (n) (m)
ferry

fête (n) (f)
festival, celebration

feu (n) (m)
fire

feu d'artifice (n) (m)
firework

feuille (n) (f)
leaf

feutre (n) (m)
felt-tip pen

feux de signalisation
(n) (m)
traffic lights

ficelle (n) (f)
string

fier/fière (adj)
proud

fille (n) (f)
daughter, girl

film (n) (m)
film

fils (n) (m)
son

fin (n) (f)
end (final part)

fin/fine (adj)
thin

flamme (n) (f)
flame

flèche (n) (f)
arrow

fleur (n) (f)
flower

flocon de neige (n) (m)
snowflake

flûte (n) (f)
flute

foin (n) (m)
hay

foire (n) (f)
fair

foncé/foncée (adj)
dark (hair)

fond (n) (m)
bottom

fontaine (n) (f)
fountain

football (n) (m)
soccer (game)

forêt (n) (f)
forest

forêt tropicale (n) (f)
rain forest

forme (n) (f)
shape

formidable (adj)
great

fort/forte (adj)
strong

fou/folle (adj)
mad

foule (n) (f)
crowd

four (n) (m)
oven

fourchette (n) (f)
fork

fourmi (n) (f)
ant

frais/fraîche (adj)
cool, fresh

fraise (n) (f)
strawberry

framboise (n) (f)
raspberry

français (n) (m)
French

frère (n) (m)
brother

frisé/frisée (adj)
curly

frites (n) (f)
chips

froid/froide (adj)
cold

fromage (n) (m)
cheese

fruit (n) (m)
fruit

fruits de mer (n) (m)
seafood

fumée (n) (f)
smoke

fusée (n) (f)
rocket, space rocket

G

gagnant/gagnante (n)
(m/f)
winner

galaxie (n) (f)
galaxy

galet (n) (m)
pebble

gant (n) (m)
glove

gant de cuisine (n) (m)
oven mitt

garage (n) (m)
garage

garçon (n) (m)
boy

A
B
C
D
E
F
G
H
I
J
K
L
M
N
O
P
Q
R
S
T
U
V
W
X
Y
Z

A
B
C
D
E
F
G
H
I
J
K
L
M
N
O
P
Q
R
S
T
U
V
W
X
Y
Z

garçon de café (n) (m)
waiter

garde (n) (m)
guard

gare (n) (f)
railroad station

gâteau (n) (m)
cake

gâteau d'anniversaire
(n) (m)
birthday cake

gauche (adj)
left

gaucher/gauchère
(adj)
left-handed

gaz (n) (m)
gas

gazeux/gazeuse (adj)
carbonated

géant (n) (m)
giant

gelé/gelée (adj)
frozen

genou (n) (m)
knee

gens (n) (m)
people

gentil/gentille (adj)
kind (gentle)

géographie (n) (f)
geography

gilet de sauvetage
(n) (m)
life jacket

girafe (n) (f)
giraffe

glace (n) (f)
ice, ice cream

glacial/glaciale (adj)
frosty (weather)

glacier (n) (m)
glacier

glaçon (n) (m)
ice cube

glissant/glissante
(adj)
slippery

globe (n) (m)
globe

golf (n) (m)
golf

gomme (n) (f)
eraser

gorge (n) (f)
throat

gorille (n) (m)
gorilla

goutte (n) (f)
drop

gouvernement (n) (m)
government

graine (n) (f)
seed

grand/grande (adj)
big, tall

grand-mère (n) (f)
grandmother

grand-père (n) (m)
grandfather

grands-parents (n) (m)
grandparents

grand vent (n) (m)
gale

grange (n) (f)
barn

gratte-ciel (n) (m)
skyscraper

grenier (n) (m)
attic

grenouille (n) (f)
frog

griffe (n) (f)
claw

grille-pain (n) (m)
toaster

grippe (n) (f)
flu

gris/grise (adj)
gray

gros/grosse (adj)
big, fat

grotte (n) (f)
cave

groupe (n) (m)
group

grue (n) (f)
crane

guépard (n) (m)
cheetah

guêpe (n) (f)
wasp

guerre (n) (f)
war

guide (n) (m)
guide

guide (n) (m)
guidebook

guitare (n) (f)
guitar

gymnastique (n) (f)
gymnastics

H

habitat (n) (m)
habitat

habitude (n) (f)
habit

hamster (n) (m)
hamster

hanche (n) (f)
hip

handicapé/handicapée
(adj)
disabled

haricots (n) (m)
beans

haut/haute (adj)
high

haut-parleur (n) (m)
loudspeaker

hélicoptère (n) (m)
helicopter (n)

hélicoptère de police
(n) (m)
police helicopter

herbe (n) (f)
grass

héron (n) (m)
heron

héros (n) (m)
hero

heure (n) (f)
hour, time

heures d'ouverture
(n) (f)
opening hours

hibou (n) (m)
owl

hier (adv)
yesterday

hippopotame (n) (m)
hippopotamus

histoire (n) (f)
history, story

historique (adj)
historical

hiver (n) (m)
winter

hockey (n) (m)
field hockey

hockey sur glace (n) (m)
ice hockey

homme (n) (m)
male (human), man

hôpital (n) (m)
hospital

horaire (n) (m)
timetable

horloge (n) (f)
clock

horrible (adj)
horrible

hors de (prep)
out of

hot-dog (n) (m)
hot dog

hôtel (n) (m)
hotel

huile (n) (f)
oil

I

ici (adv)
here

idée (n) (f)
idea

il (pron)
he

il y a du vent
windy

île (n) (f)
island

illustration (n) (f)
illustration

ils/elles (pron)
they

image (n) (f)
picture

immobile (adj)
still

imperméable (n) (m)
raincoat

imperméable (adj)
waterproof

important/importante
(adj)
important

impossible (adj)
impossible

impression (n) (f)
printout

inconfortable (adj)
uncomfortable

incroyable (adj)
amazing

infirmière (n) (f)
nurse

A
B
C
D
E
F
G
H
I
J
K
L
M
N
O
P
Q
R
S
T
U
V
W
X
Y
Z

67

A
B
C
D
E
F
G
H
I
J
K
L
M
N
O
P
Q
R
S
T
U
V
W
X
Y
Z

information (n) (f)
information

informatique (n) (f)
IT (information technology)

ingrédient (n) (m)
ingredient

inhabituel/ inhabituelle (adj)
unusual

injuste (adj)
unfair

inondation (n) (f)
flood

insecte (n) (m)
insect

insigne (n) (m)
badge

instant (n) (m)
moment

instruction (n) (f)
instruction

instrument (n) (m)
instrument

intelligent/ intelligente (adj)
smart

intéressant/ intéressante (adj)
interesting

international/ internationale (adj)
international

Internet (n) (m)
Internet

invention (n) (f)
invention

invisible (adj)
invisible

invitation (n) (f)
invitation

invité/invitée (n) (m/f)
guest

J

jamais (adv)
never

jambe (n) (f)
leg

jardin (n) (m)
garden

jardinier/jardinière (n) (m/f)
gardener

jaune (adj)
yellow

je/j' (pron)
I

jean (n) (m)
jeans

jeu (n) (m)
game

jeu de société (n) (m)
board game

jeu électronique (n) (m)
computer game

jeu vidéo (n) (m)
video game (n)

jeune (adj)
young

Jeux olympiques (n) (m)
Olympic Games

joli/jolie (adj)
pretty

joue (n) (f)
cheek

jouet (n) (m)
toy

joueur/joueuse (n) (m/f)
player

jour (n) (m)
day

journal (n) (m)
diary, newspaper

judo (n) (m)
judo

jumeau/jumelle (n) (m/f)
twin

jumelles (n) (f)
binoculars

jungle (n) (f)
jungle

jupe (n) (f)
skirt

jus (n) (m)
juice

jus de pomme (n) (m)
apple juice

jus d'orange (n) (m)
orange juice

jusqu'à (prep)
until

juste (adj)
correct

juste (adv)
just

K

kangourou (n) (m)
kangaroo

karaté (n) (m)
karate

kilogramme (n) (m)
kilogram

kilomètre (n) (m)
kilometer

koala (n) (m)
koala

L

la/lui/l' (pron)
her

là (adv)
there

là-bas (adv)
over there

lac (n) (m)
lake

laid/laide (adj)
ugly

laine (n) (f)
wool

lait (n) (m)
milk

laitier/laitière (adj)
dairy

laitue (n) (f)
lettuce

lampe (n) (f)
lamp

lampe de poche (n) (f)
torch

langue (n) (f)
language, tongue

lapin (n) (m)
rabbit

large (adj)
wide

laser (n) (m)
laser

lavabo (n) (m)
washbasin

lave-vaisselle (n) (m)
dishwasher

le/lui/l' (pron)
him

le/la/l'/les (article)
the

le sien/la sienne (pron)
hers/his

leçon (n) (f)
lesson

lecteur de CD (n) (m)
CD player

lecteur de DVD (n) (m)
DVD player

lecture (n) (f)
reading

léger/légère (adj)
light (not heavy)

légume (n) (m)
vegetable

lent/lente (adj)
slow

lentement (adv)
slowly

léopard (n) (m)
leopard

lettre (n) (f)
letter (alphabet, mail)

leur (adj)
their

lever du soleil (n) (m)
sunrise

lèvres (n) (f)
lips

lézard (n) (m)
lizard

libellule (n) (f)
dragonfly

liberté (n) (f)
freedom

librairie (n) (f)
book store

libre (adj)
free

lièvre (n) (m)
hare

ligne (n) (f)
line

limace (n) (f)
slug

limonade (n) (f)
lemonade

lion (n) (m)
lion

lion de mer (n) (m)
sea lion (n)

liquide (n) (m)
liquid (n)

lisse (adj)
smooth

liste (n) (f)
list

liste de courses (n) (f)
grocery list

lit (n) (m)
bed

A B C D E F G H I J **K** **L** M N O P Q R S T U V W X Y Z

69

litre (n) (m)
liter

lits superposés
(n) (m)
bunk beds

livre (n) (m)
book

locomotive (n) (f)
locomotive

loi (n) (f)
law

loin (adv)
far

loisir (n) (m)
hobby

long/longue (adj)
long

losange (n) (m)
diamond (shape)

loup (n) (m)
wolf

loupe (n) (f)
magnifying glass

lourd/lourde (adj)
heavy

luge (n) (f)
sled

lumière (n) (f)
light

lune (n) (f)
moon

lunettes (n) (f)
glasses

lunettes de natation
(n) (f)
goggles

lunettes de soleil
(n) (f)
sunglasses

M

machine (n) (f)
machine

machine à laver
(n) (f)
washing machine

mâchoire (n) (f)
jaw

magasin (n) (m)
store

magazine (n) (m)
magazine

magicien/magicienne
(n) (m/f)
magician

magnétique (adj)
magnetic

magnétoscope (n) (m)
video player

maillot de bain
(n) (m)
swimsuit, trunks

main (n) (f)
hand

maintenant (adv)
now

mais (conj)
but

maison (n) (f)
home, house

maître/maîtresse
(n) (m/f)
teacher

mal (n) (m)
harm

maladroit/maladroite
(adj)
clumsy

mal de tête (n) (m)
headache

malade (adj)
ill, sick

maladie (n) (f)
illness

malheureux/
malheureuse (adj)
miserable

maman (n) (f)
mom

mammifère (n) (m)
mammal

manche (n) (f)
sleeve

manteau (n) (m)
coat

maquillage (n) (m)
makeup

marché (n) (m)
market

marée (n) (f)
tide

mari (n) (m)
husband

mariage (n) (m)
marriage

marié/mariée (adj)
married

marin (n) (m)
sailor

marionnette (n) (f)
puppet

marron (adj)
brown

masque (n) (m)
mask

match (n) (m)
game (soccer)

matelas (n) (m)
mattress

matériel (n) (m)
equipment

mathématiques (n) (f)
math

matin (n) (m)
morning

mauvais/mauvaise (adj)
bad, evil

mauvaise herbe (n) (f)
weed

me/moi/m' (pron)
me

méchant/méchante (adj)
nasty (unkind)

médaille (n) (f)
medal

médecin (n) (m)
doctor

médicament (n) (m)
medicine

méduse (n) (f)
jellyfish

meilleur/meilleure (adj)
better

mélange (n) (m)
mixture

melon (n) (m)
melon

même (adv)
even

même (adj)
same

mémoire (n) (f)
memory

menton (n) (m)
chin

mer (n) (f)
sea

mère (n) (f)
mother

message (n) (m)
message

mesure (n) (f)
measurement

mètre (n) (m)
tape measure

mètre (n) (m)
meter

métro (n) (m)
subway
(underground)

meubles (n) (m)
furniture

microbe (n) (m)
bug (illness)

micro-ondes (n) (m)
microwave

microscope (n) (m)
microscope

miel (n) (m)
honey

mieux (adj)
best

milieu (n) (m)
middle

milk-shake (n) (m)
milkshake

mille
thousand

milliard
billion

million
million

mince (adj)
thin (slim)

minéral (n) (m)
mineral

minuit (n) (m)
midnight

minuscule (adj)
tiny

minute (n) (f)
minute

miroir (n) (m)
mirror

mitaine (n) (f)
mitten

mode (n) (f)
fashion

mois (n) (m)
month

moisson (n) (f)
harvest

moissonneuse-batteuse (n) (f)
combine harvester

moitié (n) (f)
half

mon/ma (adj)
my

monde (n) (m)
world

monstre (n) (m)
monster

montagne (n) (f)
mountain

montgolfière (n) (f)
hot-air balloon

montre (n) (f)
watch

moquette (n) (f)
carpet

morceau (n) (m)
piece

mort/morte (adj)
dead

mosquée (n) (f)
mosque

mot (n) (m)
term, word

moteur (n) (m)
motor

motif (n) (m)
pattern

moto (n) (f)
motorcycle

mouche (n) (f)
fly

mouchoir (n) (m)
handkerchief

mouchoirs en papier (n) (m)
tissues

mouette (n) (f)
seagull

mouillé/mouillée (adj)
wet

moustache (n) (f)
moustache, whisker

moustique (n) (m)
mosquito

mouton (n) (m)
sheep

moyen/moyenne (adj)
medium

mur (n) (m)
wall

mûr/mûre (adj)
ripe

muscle (n) (m)
muscle

musée (n) (m)
museum

musicien/musicienne (n) (m/f)
musician

musique (n) (f)
music

N

n'importe qui (pron)
anybody

n'importe quoi (pron)
anything

nageoire (n) (f)
fin

narine (n) (f)
nostril

natation (n) (f)
swimming

nature (n) (f)
nature

navire (n) (m)
ship

neige (n) (f)
snow

nénuphar (n) (m)
water lily

nerfs (n) (m)
nerves

neveu (n) (m)
nephew

nez (n) (m)
nose

nid (n) (m)
nest

nièce (n) (f)
niece

Noël (n) (m)
Christmas

nœud (n) (m)
knot

noir/noire (adj)
black

nom (n) (m)
name

nom de famille (n) (m)
last name

nombre (n) (m)
number

non (adv)
no

nord (n) (m)
north

note (n) (f)
mark

notre (adj)
our

nouilles (n) (f)
noodles

nourriture (n) (f)
food

nous (pron)
we

nouveau/nouvelle (adj)
new

nouvelles (n) (f)
news

nuage (n) (m)
cloud

nuageux/nuageuse (adj)
cloudy

nuit (n) (f)
night

nulle part (adv)
nowhere

O

oasis (n) (f)
oasis

objet (n) (m)
object

occupé/occupée (adj)
busy

océan (n) (m)
ocean

odeur (n) (f)
smell

œil (n) (m)
eye

œuf (n) (m)
egg

oignon (n) (m)
onion

oiseau (n) (m)
bird

oiseau-mouche (n) (m)
hummingbird

ombre (n) (f)
shadow

oncle (n) (m)
uncle

ongle (n) (m)
nail

opération (n) (f)
operation

or (n) (m)
gold

orage (n) (m)
thunderstorm

orageux/orageuse (adj)
stormy

orange (adj)
orange (color)

orange (n) (f)
orange (fruit)

orchestre (n) (m)
orchestra

ordinateur (n) (m)
computer

ordinateur portable (n) (m)
laptop

ordures (n) (f)
rubbish

oreille (n) (f)
ear

oreiller (n) (m)
pillow

orteil (n) (m)
toe

os (n) (m)
bone

otite (n) (f)
earache

ou (conj)
or

où (adv)
where

ouest (n) (m)
west

oui (adv)
yes

ouragan (n) (m)
hurricane

ours (n) (m)
bear

ours blanc (n) (m)
polar bear

ours en peluche (n) (m)
teddy bear

outil (n) (m)
tool

ouvert/ouverte (adj)
open

ouvrier/ouvrière (n) (m/f)
construction worker

ovale (n) (m)
oval

oxygène (n) (m)
oxygen

P

page (n) (f)
page

paille (n) (f)
drinking straw, straw

pain (n) (m)
bread

A B C D E F G H I J K L M N O P Q R S T U V W X Y Z

paire (n) (f)
pair

paix (n) (f)
peace

pâle (adj)
pale

palme (n) (f)
flipper

palmier (n) (m)
palm tree

panda (n) (m)
panda

panier (n) (m)
basket

panier repas (n) (m)
lunch box

panneau (n) (m)
board (notice), sign

pantalon (n) (m)
pants

pantoufle (n) (f)
slipper

papa (n) (m)
dad

papier (n) (m)
paper

papier toilette (n) (m)
toilet paper

papillon (n) (m)
butterfly

papillon de nuit (n) (m)
moth

pâquerette (n) (f)
daisy

parachute (n) (m)
parachute

parapluie (n) (m)
umbrella (for rain)

parasol (n) (m)
umbrella (for sun)

parc (n) (m)
park

parce que (conj)
because

parent (n) (m)
parent

paresseux/paresseuse
(adj)
lazy

parfait/parfaite (adj)
perfect

particulier/
particulière (adj)
special

partie (n) (f)
part

partout (adv)
everywhere

pas (n) (m)
step

passage clouté (n) (m)
crosswalk

passager/passagère
(n) (m/f)
passenger

passé (n) (m)
past (history)

passeport (n) (m)
passport

pastèque (n) (f)
watermelon

pâte à modeler (n) (f)
modeling clay

pâtes (n) (f)
pasta

patient/patiente (adj)
patient

patient/patiente (n) (m/f)
patient

patins à roulettes (n) (m)
rollerskates

patinage sur glace
(n) (m)
ice skating

patte (n) (f)
foot (animal), paw

pause (n) (f)
break

pauvre (adj)
poor

pays (n) (m)
country

PC (n) (m)
personal computer

peau (n) (f)
skin

pêche (n) (f)
fishing

pédale (n) (f)
pedal

peigne (n) (m)
comb

peinture (n) (f)
paint

pélican (n) (m)
pelican

pelle (n) (f)
shovel

pelouse (n) (f)
lawn

pendant (prep)
during

pendant que (conj)
while

pensée (n) (f)
thought

perdu/perdue (adj)
lost

père (n) (m)
father

perle (n) (f)
bead, pearl

perroquet (n) (m)
parrot

perruque (n) (f)
wig

personne (pron)
nobody

personne (n) (f)
person

personne âgée (n) (f)
old person

pesanteur (n) (f)
gravity

petit/petite (adj)
little, small

petit ami (m)
boyfriend

petite-fille (n) (f)
granddaughter

petit-déjeuner (n) (m)
breakfast

petit-fils (n) (m)
grandson

petit pain (m)
(bread) roll

petit pois (m)
pea

petits-enfants (n) (m)
grandchildren

petit tapis (m)
mat

petite amie (f)
girlfriend

peu profond/
peu profonde (adj)
shallow

peut-être (adv)
maybe, perhaps

phare (n) (m)
lighthouse

pharmacie (n) (f)
chemist

phoque (n) (m)
seal

photo (n) (f)
photo

piano (n) (m)
piano

pièce (n) (f)
coin, room

pièce de théâtre (n) (f)
play

pied (n) (m)
foot

pierre (n) (f)
stone

pieuvre (n) (f)
octopus

pile (n) (f)
battery

pilote (n) (m)
pilot

pin (n) (m)
pine tree

pinceau (n) (m)
paint brush

pingouin (n) (m)
penguin

pique-nique (n) (m)
picnic

pirate (n) (m)
pirate

pire (adj)
worst

piscine (n) (f)
swimming pool

pissenlit (n) (m)
dandelion

piste (n) (f)
runway

pizza (n) (f)
pizza

placard (n) (m)
cupboard

plafond (n) (m)
ceiling

plage (n) (f)
beach

plan (n) (m)
plan

planche de surf (n) (f)
surfboard

planète (n) (f)
planet

plante (n) (f)
plant

plat/plate (adj)
flat, level

A
B
C
D
E
F
G
H
I
J
K
L
M
N
O
P
Q
R
S
T
U
V
W
X
Y
Z

plateau (n) (m)
tray

plein/pleine (adj)
full

plongée (n) (f)
diving

pluie (n) (f)
rain

plume (n) (f)
feather

plus que
more than

pneu (n) (m)
tire

poche (n) (f)
pocket

poêle (n) (f)
frying pan

poids (n) (m)
weight

poignet (n) (m)
wrist

poils (n) (m)
fur

poilu/poilue (adj)
hairy

point (n) (m)
point

pointu/pointue (adj)
pointed

poire (n) (f)
pear

poisson (n) (m)
fish

poisson rouge (n) (m)
goldfish

poitrine (n) (f)
chest

poivre (n) (m)
pepper

polaire (n) (f)
fleece

poli/polie (adj)
polite

police (n) (f)
police

policier (n) (m)
femme policier (n) (m)
police officer

pollution (n) (f)
pollution

pomme (n) (f)
apple

pomme de pin (n) (f)
pinecone

pomme de terre (n) (f)
potato

pompier (n) (m)
firefighter

poney (n) (m)
pony

pont (n) (m)
bridge, deck (boat)

populaire (adj)
popular

population (n) (f)
population

port (n) (m)
harbor, port

porte (n) (f)
door

porte d'entrée (n) (f)
front door

portefeuille (n) (m)
wallet

porte-monnaie (n) (m)
change purse

portrait (n) (m)
portrait

position (n) (f)
position

possible (adj)
possible

poste (n) (f)
mail

pot de peinture (n) (m)
paint can

potage (n) (m)
soup

poteau (n) (m)
pole

poterie (n) (f)
pottery

poubelle (n) (f)
bin

pouce (n) (m)
thumb

poudre (n) (f)
powder

poulet (n) (m)
chicken

poumon (n) (m)
lung

poupée (n) (f)
doll

pourquoi (adv)
why

poussette (n) (f)
buggy

poussière (n) (f)
dust

poussin (n) (m)
chick

préféré/préférée (adj)
favorite

premier/première (adj)
first

premiers secours (n) (m)
first aid

préparatifs (n) (m)
preparations

près de (prep)
near

présentation (n) (f)
introduction

président/e (n) (m/f)
president

presque (adv)
almost, nearly

prêt/prête (adj)
ready

prince (n) (m)
prince

princesse (n) (f)
princess

principal/principale (adj)
main

printemps (n) (m)
spring (season)

prise électrique (n) (f)
plug (electric)

privé/privée (adj)
private

prix (n) (m)
price, prize

probablement (adv)
probably

problème (n) (m)
problem

prochain/prochaine (adj)
next

proche (adj)
close (near)

profond/profonde (adj)
deep

proie (n) (f)
prey

projet (n) (m)
project

promenade (n) (f)
walk

propre (adj)
clean, own

prudent/prudente (adj)
careful

prune (n) (f)
plum

public/publique (adj)
public

puce (n) (f)
microchip

puissant/puissante (adj)
powerful

pull (n) (m)
sweater

pull-over (n) (m)
sweater

punaise (n) (f)
thumbtack

puzzle (n) (m)
puzzle, jigsaw

pyjama (n) (m)
pajamas

pyramide (n) (f)
pyramid

Q

quai (n) (m)
platform

quand (adv)
when

quantité (n) (f)
amount/quantity

quart (n) (m)
quarter

quelque chose (pron)
something

quelquefois (adv)
sometimes

quelque part (adv)
somewhere

quelques (adj)
some

quelqu'un (pron)
someone

question (n) (f)
question

queue (n) (f)
line, tail

qui (pron)
who

quiz (n) (m)
quiz

A
B
C
D
E
F
G
H
I
J
K
L
M
N
O
P
Q
R
S
T
U
V
W
X
Y
Z

R

racine (n) (f)
root

radio (n) (f)
radio

radiographie (n) (f)
X-ray

raide (adj)
steep, straight (hair)

raisin (n) (m)
grape

rame (n) (f)
oar

ranch (n) (m)
ranch

rangée (n) (f)
row (line)

rapide (adj)
fast

raquette (n) (f)
racket

rare (adj)
rare

rat (n) (m)
rat

râteau (n) (m)
rake

rayures (n) (f)
stripes

réalité virtuelle (n) (f)
virtual reality

recette (n) (f)
recipe

récolte (n) (f)
crop

récompense (n) (f)
reward

récréation (n) (f)
playtime

rectangle (n) (m)
rectangle

réel/réelle (adj)
real

réfrigérateur (n) (m)
refrigerator

région (n) (f)
area

règle (n) (f)
ruler (measuring)

reine (n) (f)
queen

religion (n) (f)
religion

renard (n) (m)
fox

repas (n) (m)
meal

répétition (n) (f)
practice

réponse (n) (f)
answer

requin (n) (m)
shark

réserve (n) (f)
safari park

restaurant (n) (m)
restaurant

rêve (n) (m)
dream

réveil (n) (m)
alarm clock

réverbère (n) (m)
street light

rhinocéros (n) (m)
rhinoceros

rhume (n) (m)
cold

riche (adj)
rich

rien (pron)
nothing

rideau (n) (m)
curtain

rigolo (adj)
fun

rive (n) (f)
bank (river)

rivière (n) (f)
river

riz (n) (m)
rice

robe (n) (f)
dress

robinet (n) (m)
faucet

robot (n) (m)
robot

rocher (n) (m)
rock

roi (n) (m)
king

rollerblades (n) (m)
in-line skates

rond/ronde (adj)
round

rose (adj)
pink

rose (n) (f)
rose

roue (n) (f)
wheel

roue (n) (f)
cartwheel
(movement)

rouge (adj)
red

rougeole (n) (f)
measles

route (n) (f)
road

ruban (n) (m)
ribbon

ruche (n) (f)
hive

rue (n) (f)
street

rugby (n) (m)
rugby

rugueux/rugueuse (adj)
rough

ruisseau (n) (m)
stream

S

s'il te plaît/s'il vous plaît
please

sable (n) (m)
sand

sabot (n) (m)
hoof

sac (n) (m)
bag, sack,
shopping bag

sac à dos (n) (m)
backpack

sac à main (n) (m)
handbag

sac de couchage (n) (m)
sleeping bag

sac en plastique (n) (m)
plastic bag

sage (adj)
wise

saison (n) (f)
season

salade (n) (f)
salad

salade de fruits (n) (f)
fruit salad

salaire (n) (m)
pay

sale (adj)
dirty

salle à manger (n) (f)
dining room

salle de bain (n) (f)
bathroom

salle de classe (n) (f)
classroom

salon (n) (m)
living room

salut
hi

sandale (n) (f)
sandal

sandwich (n) (m)
sandwich

sang (n) (m)
blood

sans (prep)
without

saucisse (n) (f)
sausage

sauterelle (n) (f)
grasshopper

savon (n) (m)
soap

scarabée (n) (m)
beetle

scène (n) (f)
stage (theater)

sciences (n) (f)
science

scientifique (n) (m/f)
scientist

score (n) (m)
score

seau (n) (m)
bucket

sec/sèche (adj)
dry

seconde (n) (f)
second (time)

secours (n) (m)
rescue

secret (n) (m)
secret

sel (n) (m)
salt

selle (n) (f)
saddle

semaine (n) (f)
week

sens (n) (m)
meaning

A
B
C
D
E
F
G
H
I
J
K
L
M
N
O
P
Q
R
S
T
U
V
W
X
Y
Z

79

séparément (adv)
apart

serpent (n) (m)
snake

serre (n) (f)
greenhouse

serré/serrée (adj)
tight

serrure (n) (f)
lock

serveuse (n) (f)
waitress

serviette (n) (f)
towel

serviette de toilette (n) (f)
washcloth

seul/seule (adj)
alone

seulement (adv)
only

sévère (adj)
strict

shampooing (n) (m)
shampoo

short (n) (m)
shorts

siège (n) (m)
seat

sifflement (n) (m)
whistle

silence (n) (m)
silence

silencieux/silencieuse (adj)
quiet

singe (n) (m)
monkey, ape

site web (n) (m)
website

skate-board (n) (m)
skateboard

ski (n) (m)
skiing

snowboard (n) (m)
snowboard

sœur (n) (f)
sister

soir (n) (m)
evening

sol (n) (m)
floor

soldat/femme soldat (n) (m/f)
soldier

soleil (n) (m)
sun

solide (n) (m)
solid

sombre (adj)
dark

son/sa (adj)
her/his/its

son (n) (m)
sound (noise)

sorte (n) (f)
kind (type)

sortie (n) (f)
way out, exit

souffle (n) (m)
breath

souhait (n) (m)
wish

soupe (n) (f)
soup

sourcil (n) (m)
eyebrow

sourd/sourde (adj)
deaf

sourire (n) (m)
smile

souris (n) (f)
mouse (animal, computer)

sous (prep)
under, beneath

sous-marin (n) (m)
submarine

sous-vêtements (n) (m)
underwear

souvenir (n) (m)
souvenir

souvent (adv)
often

spaghettis (n) (m)
spaghetti

spectacle (n) (m)
show

spectateurs (n) (m)
audience

sport (n) (m)
sport

squelette (n) (m)
skeleton

stade (n) (m)
stadium

steak (n) (m)
steak

studio (n) (m)
studio

stupide (adj)
stupid

stylo (n) (m)
pen

sucre (n) (m)
sugar

sud (n) (m)
south

sujet (n) (m)
subject

supermarché (n) (m)
supermarket

supplémentaire (adj)
extra

sur (prep)
about, on top of

sûr/sûre (adj)
sure

surf (n) (m)
surfing

surface (n) (f)
surface

surnom (n) (m)
nickname

surprise (n) (f)
surprise

surveillant de aignade
(n) (m)
lifeguard

survêtement (n) (m)
tracksuit

sweat-shirt (n) (m)
sweatshirt

sympathique (adj)
nice

T

table (n) (f)
table

tableau (n) (m)
picture

tableau (n) (m)
blackboard

tablier (n) (m)
apron

tache de rousseur (n) (f)
freckle

taches (n) (f)
spots

taille (n) (f)
size, waist

talon (n) (m)
heel

tante (n) (f)
aunt

tapis (n) (m)
rug

tapis de souris (n) (m)
mouse mat

tasse (n) (m)
cup, mug

taxi (n) (m)
taxi

tee-shirt (n) (m)
T-shirt

télécommande (n) (f)
remote control

téléphone (n) (m)
phone (n)

téléphone portable
(n) (m)
cell phone

télescope (n) (m)
telescope

télévision (n) (f)
television

télévision par satellite
(n) (f)
satellite TV

température (n) (f)
temperature

temps (n) (m)
weather

temps libre (n) (m)
free time

tennis (n) (m)
tennis

tennis de table (n) (m)
table tennis

tente (n) (f)
tent

terrain (n) (m)
land

Terre (n) (f)
Earth (planet)

terre (n) (f)
ground, soil

terrible (adj)
terrible

têtard (n) (m)
tadpole

tête (n) (f)
head

texto (n) (m)
text message

thé (n) (m)
tea

théâtre (n) (m)
theater

A B C D E F G H I J K L M N O P Q R (S) **T** U V W X Y Z

thermomètre (n) (m)
thermometer

ticket de caisse (n) (m)
receipt

tige (n) (f)
stem

tigre (n) (m)
tiger

timbre (n) (m)
stamp

timide (adj)
shy

tiroir (n) (m)
drawer

tissu (n) (m)
cloth

toilettes (n) (f)
toilet

toit (n) (m)
roof

tomate (n) (f)
tomato

tondeuse à gazon (n) (f)
lawn mower

torchon (n) (m)
dishtowel

tornade (n) (f)
tornado

tortue (n) (f)
tortoise

tortue de mer (n) (f)
turtle

tôt (adv)
early

toucan (n) (m)
toucan

toujours (adv)
always

touriste (n) (m/f)
tourist

tournant (n) (m)
turn (bend)

tournesol (n) (m)
sunflower

tourniquet (n) (m)
traffic circle

tous (adj)
every

tous les jours (adv)
everyday

tout (pron)
everything

tout/toute (adj)
all

tout à coup (adv)
suddenly

tout de suite (adv)
immediately

tout le monde (pron)
everybody

toux (n) (f)
cough

tracteur (n) (m)
tractor

train (n) (m)
train

traîneau (n) (m)
sleigh

trajet (n) (m)
route

trampoline (n) (m)
trampoline

tranquille (adj)
peaceful

tranquillement (adv)
quietly

transport (n) (m)
transportation

travail (n) (m)
work

tremblement de terre (n) (m)
earthquake

très (adv)
very

triangle (n) (m)
triangle

triste (adj)
sad

troisième (adj)
third

trombone (n) (m)
paper clip

trompe (n) (f)
trunk (animal)

tronc (n) (m)
trunk (tree)

trône (n) (m)
throne

tropical/tropicale (adj)
tropical

trottoir (n) (m)
sidewalk

trou (n) (m)
hole

troupeau (n) (m)
flock (of sheep)

trousse (n) (f)
pencil case

tu/vous (pron)
you

tube (n) (m)
tube

tunnel (n) (m)
tunnel

U

un/une (article)
a, an

une fois (adv)
once

uniforme (n) (m)
uniform

uniforme scolaire (n) (m)
school uniform

univers (n) (m)
universe

université (n) (f)
university

urgence (n) (f)
emergency

usine (n) (f)
factory

utile (adj)
useful

V

vacances (n) (f)
vacation

vache (n) (f)
cow

vague (n) (f)
wave

vaisselle (n) (f)
dishes (dirty)

valise (n) (f)
suitcase

vallée (n) (f)
valley

vautour (n) (m)
vulture

veau (n) (m)
calf

vedette de cinéma (n) (f)
movie star

végétarien/végétarienne (n) (m/f)
vegetarian

vélo (n) (m)
bike

vendeur/vendeuse (n) (m/f)
shop assistant

vent (n) (m)
wind

ventre (n) (m)
tummy

ver (n) (m)
worm

ver de terre (n) (m)
earthworm

verbe (n) (m)
verb

vérité (n) (f)
truth

verre (n) (m)
glass (drink)

vers (prep)
toward

vert/verte (adj)
green

vêtements (n) (m)
clothes

vétérinaire (n) (m/f)
vet

viande (n) (f)
meat

vide (adj)
empty

vie (n) (f)
life

vieux/vieille (adj)
old

vilain/vilaine (adj)
bad

village (n) (m)
village

ville (n) (f)
city, town

violet/violette (adj)
purple

violon (n) (m)
violin

visage (n) (m)
face

vite (adv)
quickly

vitesse (n) (f)
speed

vivant/vivante (adj)
alive

vocabulaire (n) (m)
vocabulary

voile (n) (f)
sail

voisin/voisine (n) (m/f)
neighbor

A
B
C
D
E
F
G
H
I
J
K
L
M
N
O
P
Q
R
S
T
U
V
W
X
Y
Z

voiture (n) (f)
car

voiture de course (n) (f)
race car

voiture de police (n) (f)
police car

voix (n) (f)
voice

vol (n) (m)
flight

votre (adj)
your

voyage (n) (m)
journey, trip

vrai/vraie (adj)
true

vraiment (adv)
really

V. T. T. (n) (m)
mountain bike

zéro (n) (m)
zero

zone (n) (f)
zone

zoo (n) (m)
zoo

W

week-end (n) (m)
weekend

Y

yacht (n) (m)
yacht

yaourt (n) (m)
yogurt

Z

zèbre (n) (m)
zebra

A B C D E F G H I J K L M N O P Q R S T U V W X Y Z

Verbs

This section gives a list of useful verbs (doing words). Each verb is given in the infinitive (to...) of the verb. The most useful verbs, such as "to be" **être** and "to have" **avoir**, are written out so that you can see how they change depending on who is doing the action.

I = **je**
you = **tu**
he/she = **il/elle**
we = **nous**
you (plural/formal) = **vous**
they = **ils/elles**

We have also written out three of the most regular French verbs (**donner**, to give; **finir**, to finish; and **vendre**, to sell), so you can see how these change. A reflexive verb is also written out. Reflexive verbs are often used where you would say "myself" or "yourself" in English. An example is **se laver** (to wash oneself). The verbs that are written out are shown in the present tense—they describe what is happening now.

to act
faire du théâtre
fair dew tay-a-truh

to agree
être d'accord
eh-truh da-kor

to allow
permettre
pair-met-truh

to appear
apparaître
ap-par-eh-truh

to ask
demander
duh-mahn-day

to bake
faire de la pâtisserie
fair duh la paht-eess-ree

to bark
aboyer
ab-wa-yay

. . . .

to be
être
eh-truh

I am
je suis

you are
tu es

he, she is
il, elle est

we are
nous sommes

you (plural) are
vous êtes

they are
ils, elles sont

. . . .

to be able
pouvoir
poov-wahr

to be born
être né
eh-truh nay

to be called (named)
être appelé
eh-truh ap-play

to be cold
avoir froid
av-wahr frwa

to be hungry
avoir faim
av-wahr fa(m)

to be scared of
avoir peur de
av-wahr puhr duh

to be thirsty
avoir soif
av-wahr swaf

to become
devenir
duh-vuh-neer

to begin
commencer
kom-ahn-say

to behave
se comporter
suh kom-por-tay

to believe
croire
krwahr

to bend
plier
plee-yay

to bird-watch
observer les oiseaux
ob-zair-vay layz wa-zoh

to bite
croquer
kro-kay

to block
bloquer
blo-kay

to blow
gonfler
gon-flay

to boil
bouillir
boo-yeer

to borrow
emprunter
ahm-pran-tay

to bounce
rebondir
ruh-bon-deer

to brake
freiner
fray-nay

to break
casser
kah-say

to breathe
respirer
ruh-speer-ay

to bring
apporter
ap-por-tay

to brush
brosser
bros-say

to brush one's teeth
se brosser les dents
suh bros-say lay dah(n)

to build
construire
kon-strweer

to bump into
rentrer dans
rahn-tray dah(n)

to buy
acheter
ash-tay

to camp
camper
kahm-pay

to carry
porter
por-tay

to catch
attraper
at-tra-pay

to cause
causer
koh-zay

to celebrate
célébrer
say-lay-bray

to change
changer
shahn-zhay

to charge (a phone)
recharger
ruh-shar-zhay

to check
vérifier
vair-eef-yay

to choose
choisir
shwa-zeer

to clap your hands
taper tes main
ta-pay day ma(n)

to clean
nettoyer
net-wa-yay

to clean up
ranger
rahn-zhay

to clear (a table)
débarrasser
day-bar-ra-say

to climb
grimper
gram-pay

to close
fermer
fair-may

to collect
collectionner
kol-lek-syo-nay

to come
venir
vuh-neer

to come back
revenir
ruh-vuh-neer

to come from
venir de
vuh-neer duh

to compare
comparer
kom-pa-ray

to complain
se plaindre
suh plan-druh

to contain
contenir
kon-tuh-neer

to continue
continuer
kon-teen-ew-ay

to cook
cuisiner
kwee-zee-nay

to copy
copier
kop-yay

to cost
coûter
koo-tay

to cough
tousser
too-say

to count
compter
kom-tay

to cover
couvrir
koov-reer

to crack
casser
kass-say

to crash
s'écraser
say-krah-zay

to create
créer
kray-ay

to cross
traverser
tra-vair-say

to cry
pleurer
pluhr-ay

to cut
couper
koo-pay

to cut out
découper
day-koo-pay

to cycle
faire du vélo
fair dew vay-lo

to dance
danser
dahn-say

to decide
décider
day-see-day

to decorate
décorer
day-ko-ray

to describe
décrire
day-kreer

to destroy
détruire
day-trweer

to die
mourir
moo-reer

to dig
creuser
kruh-zay

to disappear
disparaître
dees-par-eh-truh

to discover
découvrir
day-koov-reer

to dive
plonger
plon-jay

....

to do
faire
fair

I do
je fais

you do
tu fais

he/she does
il/elle fait

we do
nous faisons

you (plural) do
vous faites

they do
ils/elles font
....

to do one's homework
faire ses devoirs
fair say duhv-wahr

to do the gardening
jardiner
zhar-dee-nay

to draw
dessiner
dess-ee-nay

to dream
rêver
reh-vay

to dress up
s'habiller
sa-bee-yay

to drink
boire
bwahr

to drive
conduire
kon-dweer

to dry
sécher
say-shay

to earn
gagner
gan-yay

to eat
manger
mahn-zhay

to encourage
encourager
ahn-koo-ra-zhay

to enjoy
aimer
eh-may

A B C D E F G H I J K L M N O P Q R S T U V W X Y Z

A
B
C
D
E
F
G
H
I
J
K
L
M
N
O
P
Q
R
S
T
U
V
W
X
Y
Z

to escape
s'échapper
say-shap-pay

to explain
expliquer
eks-plee-kay

to explode
exploser
ek-sploh-zay

to face
affronter
af-fron-tay

to fall
tomber
tom-bay

to fall down
s'écrouler
say-kroo-lay

to feed
nourrir
noo-reer

to feel
ressentir
ruh-sahn-teer

to feel unwell
ne pas se sentir bien
nuh pah suh sahn-teer bya(n)

to fetch
aller chercher
al-lay shair-shay

to fight
se battre
suh bat-truh

to fill
remplir
rahm-pleer

to find
trouver
troo-vay

to find out
se renseigner sur
suh rahn-sen-yay soor

to finish
finir
feen-eer

I finish
je finis

you finish
tu finis

he/she finishes
il/elle finit

we finish
nous finissons

you finish
vous finissez

they finish
ils/elles finissent

to float
flotter
flot-tay

to fly
voler
vo-lay

to fold
plier
plee-yay

to follow
suivre
sweev-ruh

to forget
oublier
oo-blee-yay

to freeze
geler
zhuh-lay

to frighten
effrayer
eh-fray-yay

to get
recevoir
ruh-suhv-wahr

to get on (a bus)
monter
mon-tay

to get ready
se préparer
suh pray-pa-ray

to get up
se lever
suh le-vay

to give
donner
don-nay

I give
je donne

you give
tu donnes

he/she gives
il/elle donne

we give
nous donnons

you (plural) give
vous donnez

they give
ils/elles donnent

to go
aller
ah-lay

I go
je vais

you go
tu vas

he/she goes
il/elle va

we go
nous allons

you (plural) go
vous allez

they go
ils/elles vont

to go camping
faire du camping
fair dew kahm-peeng

to go home
rentrer
rahn-tray

to go on vacation
partir en vacances
par-teer ah(n) vak-ahns

to go out
sortir
sor-teer

to go shopping
faire les courses
fair lay koorss

to grow
pousser
poo-say

to guess
deviner
duh-vee-nay

to hang up (a phone)
raccrocher
rak-ro-shay

to happen
arriver
ar-ree-vay

to hate
détester
day-tes-tay

....

to have
avoir
av-wahr

I have
j'ai

you have
tu as

he/she has
il/elle a

we have
nous avons

you (plural) have
vous avez

they have
ils/elles ont

....

to have breakfast
prendre le
petit-déjeuner
*prahn-druh luh puh-tee
day-zhuh-nay*

to have fun
s'amuser
sam-ew-zay

to have lunch
déjeuner
day-zhuh-nay

to have to
devoir
duhv-wahr

to hear
entendre
ahn-tahn-druh

to help
aider
eh-day

to hide
cacher
ka-shay

to hit
frapper
frap-pay

to hold
tenir
tuh-neer

to hop
sauter
soh-tay

to hope
espérer
es-pair-ay

to hurry
se dépêcher
suh day-peh-shay

to hurt
blesser
bless-ay

to imagine
imaginer
ee-ma-zhee-nay

to include
inclure
an-klewr

to inspire
inspirer
an-spee-ray

to invent
inventer
an-vahn-tay

to invite
inviter
an-vee-tay

to join
joindre
zhwan-druh

to jump
sauter
soh-tay

to keep
garder
gar-day

to kick
donner un coup
de pied
don-nay a(n) koo duh pyay

to kill
tuer
tew-ay

to kiss
embrasser
ahm-bra-say

A
B
C
D
E
F
G
H
I
J
K
L
M
N
O
P
Q
R
S
T
U
V
W
X
Y
Z

A
B
C
D
E
F
G
H
I
J
K
L
M
N
O
P
Q
R
S
T
U
V
W
X
Y
Z

to know (someone)
connaître
kon-neh-truh

to know (something)
savoir
sav-wahr

to land (in a plane)
atterrir
at-tair-eer

to last
durer
dew-ray

to laugh
rire
reer

to leap
bondir
bon-deer

to learn
apprendre
ap-prahn-druh

to lie
mentir
mahn-teer

to lift
lever
luh-vay

to like
aimer
eh-may

to listen to
écouter
ay-koo-tay

to live
vivre
veev-ruh

to lock
fermer à clé
fair-may ah klay

to look
regarder
ruh-gar-day

to look after
s'occuper de
sok-ew-pay duh

to look for
chercher
shair-shay

to lose
perdre
pair-druh

to love
adorer
ad-or-ay

to magnify
grossir
groh-seer

to make
fabriquer
fab-ree-kay

to make a wish
faire un vœu
fair a(n) vuh

to make friends
se faire des amis
suh fair dez a-mee

to marry
se marier
suh mar-yay

to mean
signifier
seen-yeef-yay

to meet
rencontrer
rahn-kon-tray

to move
bouger
boo-zhay

to need
avoir besoin de
av-wahr buh-zwah(n) duh

to notice
remarquer
ruh-mar-kay

to offer
offrir
off-reer

to open
ouvrir
oov-reer

to own
posséder
po-say-day

to pack
faire les valises
fair lay val-eez

to paint
peindre
pan-druh

to pay
payer
pay-yay

to persuade
persuader
pair-swa-day

to pick up
ramasser
ram-ah-say

to plan
organiser
or-gan-ee-zay

to play
jouer
zhoo-ay

to play an instrument
jouer d'un
instrument
zhoo-ay dan an-strew-mah(n)

to point
indiquer
an-dee-kay

to pour
verser
vair-say

to practice
s'entraîner
sahn-treh-nay

to predict
prédire
pray-deer

to prefer
préférer
pray-fair-ay

to prepare
préparer
pray-pa-ray

to press
appuyer sur
ap-pwee-yay soor

to pretend
faire semblant
fair sahm-blah(n)

to print
imprimer
am-pree-may

to produce
produire
pro-dweer

to promise
promettre
pro-met-truh

to protect
protéger
pro-tay-zhay

to provide
fournir
foor-neer

to pull
tirer
teer-ay

to push
pousser
poo-say

to put
mettre
met-truh

to put away
ranger
rahn-zhay

to rain
pleuvoir
pluhv-wahr

to reach
atteindre
at-tan-druh

to read
lire
leer

to realize
se rendre compte
suh rahn-druh komt

to recognize
reconnaître
ruh-kon-neh-truh

to refuse
refuser
ruh-few-zay

to relax
se détendre
suh day-tahn-druh

to remain
rester
res-tay

to remember
se souvenir de
suh soo-vuh-neer duh

to repair
réparer
ray-pa-ray

to rest
se reposer
suh ruh-poh-zay

to return
revenir
ruh-vuh-neer

to ride a bike
faire du vélo
fair dew vay-lo

to ride a horse
monter à cheval
mon-tay ah shuh-val

to ring
sonner
so-nay

to roll
rouler
roo-lay

to row
se promener
en barque
suh pro-muh-nay ah(n) bark

to rub
frotter
fro-tay

to run
courir
koo-reer

to run after
poursuivre
poor-swee-vruh

to sail
faire de la voile
fair duh la vwal

to save
sauver
soh-vay

A
B
C
D
E
F
G
H
I
J
K
L
M
N
O
P
Q
R
S
T
U
V
W
X
Y
Z

to say
dire
deer

to score (a goal)
marquer
mar-kay

to scratch (oneself)
se gratter
suh grat-tay

to search
chercher
shair-shay

to see
voir
vwahr

to seem
sembler
sahm-blay

to sell
vendre
vahn-druh

I sell
je vends

you sell
tu vends

he/she sells
il/elle vend

we sell
nous vendons

you (plural) sell
vous vendez

they sell
ils/elles vendent

to send
envoyer
ahn-vwa-yay

to set a table
mettre la table
met-truh la tab-luh

to shake
agiter
azh-ee-tay

to share
partager
par-ta-zhay

to shine
briller
bree-yay

to shout
crier
kree-yay

to show
montrer
mon-tray

to sing
chanter
shahn-tay

to sit
s'asseoir
sass-wahr

to skate (on ice)
patiner (sur glace)
pa-tee-nay

to skate (roller)
faire du roller
fair dew ro-lair

to ski
skier
skee-yay

to sleep
dormir
dor-meer

to slide
glisser
glee-say

to slip
glisser
glee-say

to smell
sentir
sahn-teer

to smile
sourire
soo-reer

to snow
neiger
nay-zhay

to sound (like)
sembler
sahm-blay

to speak
parler
par-lay

to spell
épeler
ay-puh-lay

to spin
tourner
toor-nay

to spread
étaler
ay-ta-lay

to stand
se tenir debout
suh tuh-neer duh-boo

to stand up
se lever
suh luh-vay

to start
commencer
kom-ahn-say

to stay
rester
res-tay

to stick
coller
kol-lay

to sting
piquer
pee-kay

to stop
arrêter
arh-reh-tay

to stretch
s'étirer
say-teer-ay

to study
étudier
ay-tewd-yay

to surf
surfer
soor-fay

to surprise
surprendre
soor-prahn-druh

to survive
survivre
soor-veev-ruh

to swim
nager
na-zhay

to take
prendre
prahn-druh

to take a picture
prendre une photo
prahn-druh ewn fo-toh

to take away
emporter
ahm-por-tay

to take turns
faire à tour de rôle
fair ah toor duh rohl

to talk
parler
par-lay

to take a shower
prendre une douche
prahn-druh ewn doosh

to taste
goûter
goo-tay

to teach
enseigner
ahn-sen-yay

to tease
taquiner
tak-ee-nay

to tell
raconter
rak-on-tay

to tell a story
raconter une histoire
rak-on-tay ewn eest-wahr

to tell the time
dire l'heure
deer luhr

to thank
remercier
ruh-mair-syay

to think
réfléchir
ray-flay-sheer

to throw
jeter
zhuh-tay

to tie
attacher
at-ta-shay

to touch
toucher
too-shay

to train
entraîner
ahn-treh-nay

to translate
traduire
trad-weer

to travel
voyager
vwa-ya-zhay

to treat (well)
traiter (bien)
tray-tay bya(n)

to try (on)
essayer
es-say-yay

to turn
tourner
toor-nay

to type
taper
ta-pay

to understand
comprendre
kom-prahn-druh

to undress
se déshabiller
suh day-sa-bee-yay

to unpack
déballer
day-bal-lay

to use
utiliser
ew-tee-lee-zay

to visit
visiter
vee-zee-tay

to wait
attendre
at-tahn-druh

to wake up
se réveiller
suh ray-vay-yay

A B C D E F G H I J K L M N O P Q R S T U V W X Y Z

93

A
B
C
D
E
F
G
H
I
J
K
L
M
N
O
P
Q
R
S
T
U
V
W
X
Y
Z

to walk
marcher
mar-shay

to want
vouloir
vool-wahr

to warm
réchauffer
ray-shoh-fay

to wash
laver
la-vay

to wash (oneself)
se laver
suh la-vay

I wash
je me lave

you wash
tu te laves

he/she washes
il/elle se lave

we wash
nous nous lavons

you (plural) wash
vous vous lavez

they wash
ils/elles se lavent

to wash the dishes
laver la vaisselle
la-vay la vay-sel

to watch
regarder
ruh-gar-day

to wave
faire un signe de la
main
fair a(n) seen-ye duh la ma(n)

to wear
porter
por-tay

to weigh
peser
puh-zay

to whisper
chuchoter
shew-sho-tay

to win
gagner
gan-yay

to wish
souhaiter
sway-tay

to wonder
se demander
suh duh-mahn-day

to work
travailler
tra-va-yay

to work (function)
fonctionner
fonk-syo-nay

to wrap
emballer
ahm-bal-lay

to write
écrire
ay-kreer

Useful Phrases

Yes
Oui
wee

No
Non
no(n)

Hello
Bonjour
bon-zhoor

Goodbye
Au revoir
oh ruhv-wahr

See you later
À bientôt
ah byan-toh

Please
S'il te plaît
seel tuh pleh

Thank you
Merci
mair-see

Excuse me
Excuse-moi
eks-kewz mwa

I'm sorry
Je suis désolé
zhuh swee day-zo-lay

My name is...
Je m'appelle...
zhuh ma-pel

I live...
J'habite à...
zha-beet ah

I am... years old
J'ai... ans
zhay...ah(n)

I don't understand
Je ne comprends pas
zhuh nuh kom-prah(n) pah

I don't know
Je ne sais pas
zhuh nuh say pah

Very well
Très bien
treh bya(n)

Very much
Beaucoup
boh-koo

I like/I don't like
J'aime/Je n'aime pas...
zhehm/zhuh nehm pah

Let's go!
Allons-y !
alohn-zee

Happy Birthday!
Bon anniversaire!
bo(n) an-ee-vair-sair

How are you?
Comment ça va ?
ko-mah(n) sa va

What is your name?
Comment t'appelles-tu ?
ko-mah(n) ta-pel tew

Do you speak...?
Parles-tu... ?
parl tew

Do you like...?
Aimes-tu... ?
ehm tew

Do you have...?
As-tu... ?
ah tew

May I have...?
Puis-je avoir... ?
pwee zhuh av-wahr

How much...?
Combien... ?
kom-bya(n)

What's that?
Qu'est-ce que c'est?
kess kuh say

How many?
Combien?
kom-bya(n)

Can you help me?
Peux-tu m'aider?
puh tew meh-day

What time is it?
Quelle heure est-il?
kel uhr et eel

Help!
Au secours!
oh suh-koor

Stop!
Arrête!
ar-reht

Turn right/left
Tourne à droite/à gauche
toorn ah drwat/ah gohsh

Go straight on
Va tout droit
va too drwa

In front of
Devant
duh-vah(n)

Next to
À côté de
ah koh-tay duh

Where is/are...?
Où est/sont... ?
oo eh/so(n)

Monday
lundi
lahn-dee

Tuesday
mardi
mar-dee

Wednesday
mercredi
mair-kruh-dee

Thursday
jeudi
zhuh-dee

Friday
vendredi
vahn-druh-dee

Saturday
samedi
sam-dee

Sunday
dimanche
dee-mahnsh

January
janvier
zhahnv-yay

February
février
fay-vree-yay

March
mars

April
avril
av-reel

May
mai
may

June
juin
zhwa(n)

July
juillet
zhwee-yay

August
août
oot

September
septembre
sep-tahm-bruh

October
octobre
ok-to-bruh

November
novembre
no-vahm-bruh

December
décembre
day-sahm-bruh